THE TRADITIONAL ARCHITECTURE OF MEXICO

With 367 illustrations, 23 in colour

THAMES AND HUDSON

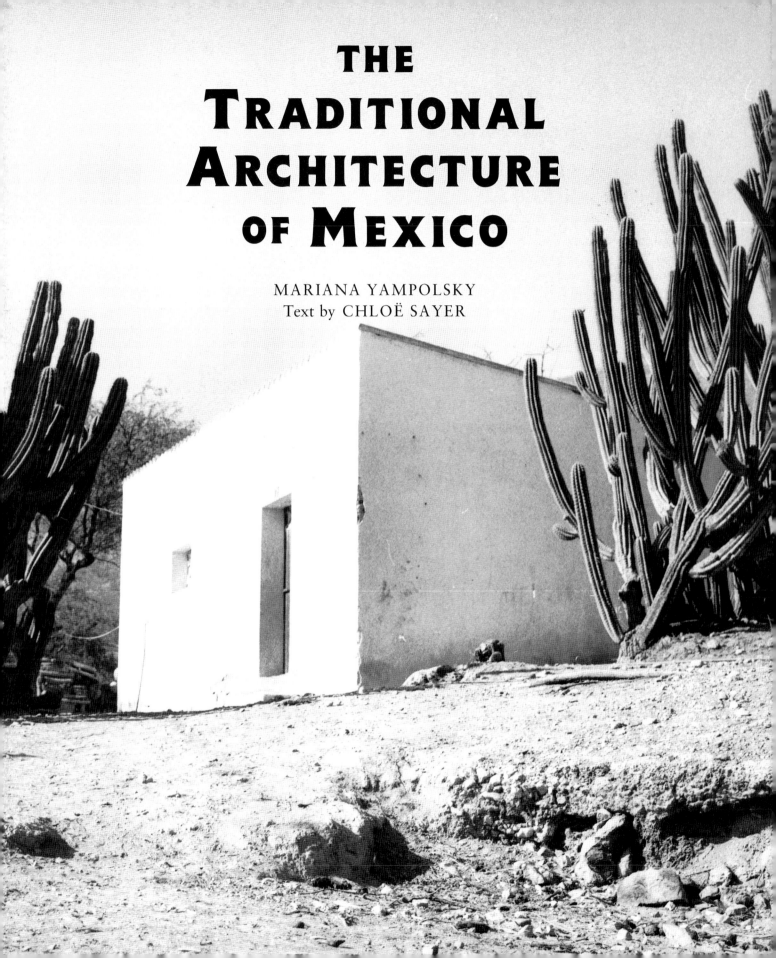

THE
TRADITIONAL
ARCHITECTURE
OF MEXICO

MARIANA YAMPOLSKY
Text by CHLOË SAYER

To the great unnamed builders of Mexico, who are the true authors of this book

ACKNOWLEDGMENTS

Mariana Yampolsky and Chloë Sayer wish to express their gratitude to Alicia Ahumada, friend and colleague, who prepared the black and white photographic prints for reproduction, to architect Jorge Huft who read the text with care and gave much valuable advice, to Fidel Figueroa Ochoa, Javier Gómez Alvarez-Tostado, Armando Bustundui, Oscar Hagerman, Doris Heyden, Ruth D. Lechuga, David Maawad, Arij Ouweneel, Jorge Ramírez, Francisco Reyes Palma and Ricardo Rendón Garcini for their help and assistance and to David Lavender and Arjen van der Sluis for their encouragement and support.

Title page   *Los Reyes Metzontla, Puebla*

British Library Cataloguing-in-Publication Data

A catalogue record for this book is available from the British Library

ISBN 0-500-34128-1

Printed and bound in Singapore

CONTENTS

Map of Mexico showing present-day states and the Tropic of Cancer. Also included here are pre-Hispanic sites referred to in the text. Mexico City was built on the ruins of Tenochtitlan, the Aztec capital.

1 Casas Grandes (Paquimé)
2 El Tajín
3 Tula
4 Teotihuacán
5 Monte Albán
6 Mitla
7 Palenque
8 Uxmal
9 Chichén Itzá
10 Uaxactun

TRADITION AND CHANGE

The city is spread out in circles of jade,
radiating flashes of light like quetzal plumes,
Beside it the lords are borne in canoes:
over them extends a flowery mist . . .

(Aztec poem, 1528)

IN 1519 THE SPANISH *conquistadores*, led by Hernán Cortés, landed on the shores of Mexico, passed between the great volcanoes, and for the first time saw Tenochtitlan, the island capital of the Aztec empire. Linked to the mainland by three causeways, it was ringed by a constellation of satellite towns. 'When we beheld so many cities and villages built in the water and other great settlements on dry land . . . we could not restrain our admiration,' wrote the soldier Bernal Díaz del Castillo. 'It was like the enchantments in the book of Amadis, on account of the great towers and temples and buildings rising from the water, and all built of masonry. Some of our soldiers even asked whether the things that we saw were not a dream.'

History and myth suggest that the Aztec, or Mexica, came originally from Aztlán, 'Place of Herons'. Guided during their long migration by Huitzilopochtli, war deity and representative of the sun, they took refuge in 1325 on a previously uninhabited and marshy island near the western edge of Lake Texcoco. Here they saw the sign that their god had promised them: an eagle poised upon a prickly pear, eating a serpent. By digging ditches to create raised areas of dry land, the Aztec made the most of their swampy and inhospitable environment. They also built *chinampas* (artificial cultivation plots) in the lake, using mounds of turf and mud-covered 'rafts' of wickerwork and branches. This agricultural system permitted multiple harvests each year; it also enabled the islanders to extend their terrain. From a cluster of reed and grass huts, Tenochtitlan evolved in under two hundred years to become one of the largest and best ordered cities in the world. Laid out on a grid, with a network of roads and canals, it covered nearly 52 square kilometres (20 sq. miles) by 1519, and accommodated between 150,000 and 300,000 inhabitants; Toledo, the royal capital of Spain, had just 18,000 inhabitants at this time.

The Aztec took great pride in their mighty metropolis, soon to be demolished by Spanish forces. Although archaeological finds continue to yield important

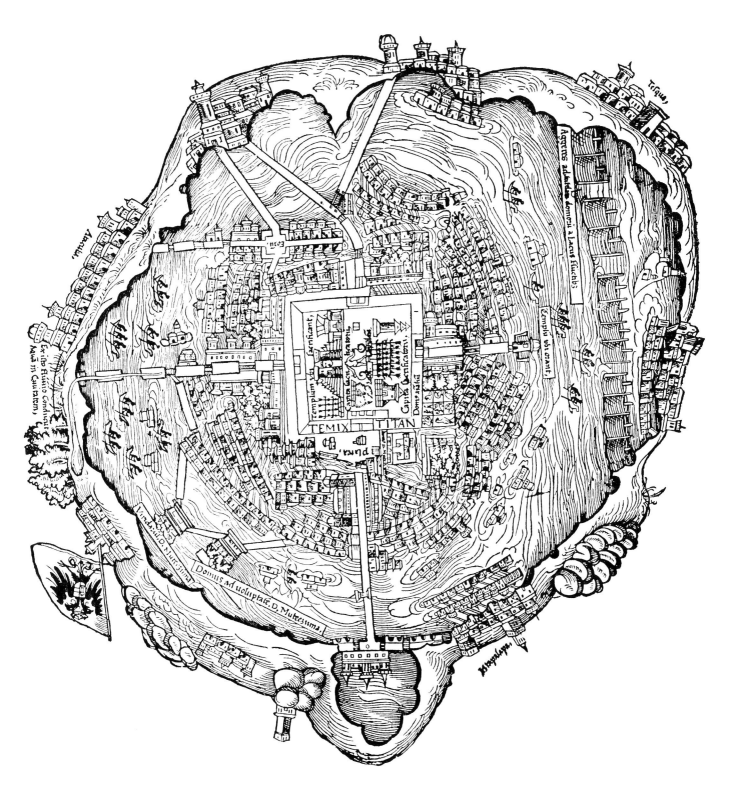

Opposite Published in Nuremberg in 1524, this map shows Tenochtitlan ('Temixtitan'), the island capital of the Aztec empire. Buildings are portrayed in a European manner. Ringed by satellite towns, the metropolis was linked to the mainland by three broad causeways running north (top), south and west; wooden drawbridges allowed waterflow and controlled access to the island. The eastern causeway terminated at the lake. Two aqueducts brought fresh water from the mainland. At the city's heart lay the sacred precinct with twin shrines dedicated to Tláloc and Huitzilopochtli.

Below Aztec temple, crowned by twin shrines. The shrine on the northern side (left) was dedicated to Tláloc, god of rain and green growth; that on the southern side (right) to Huitzilopochtli, war and sun god. Each roof consisted of a wooden frame covered with cement and lime. Tláloc's was painted with blue and white vertical stripes; Huitzilopochtli's was ornamented with carved skulls painted white on a red or black background. Each roof was extended skywards by a crest, on top of which were stylized shells, symbolizing water (left), and butterflies, symbolizing fire and sun (right).

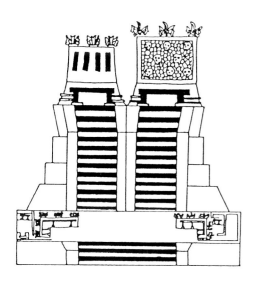

information, it is ironic that our knowledge of Tenochtitlan should chiefly rest on the descriptions left by its destroyers. Four days after their arrival in the city, Spanish soldiers followed the Aztec emperor, Moctezuma II, up the steps of the great temple of Tlatelolco. This moment was movingly evoked by Bernal Díaz del Castillo:

Moctezuma then took [Cortés] by the hand and told him to observe his great city and all the other towns nearby on the lake, and the many settlements built on dry land. . . . So we stood looking about us, for that tall and accursed temple stood so high that from it we could see over everything, and we saw the three causeways that lead into México-Tenochtitlan. . . . We saw the aqueduct that comes from Chapultepec to supply the city with fresh water, and at intervals along the three causeways the bridges which let the water flow from one part of the lake to another. We beheld on that great lake a multitude of canoes, some coming with supplies of food and others returning loaded with merchandise. . . . And we saw in those cities temples and oratories shaped like towers and fortresses, all gleaming white, a wonderful thing to behold. We saw houses with flat roofs, and along the causeways other towers and adoratories that looked like fortresses. . . . We observed the great *plaza* and the great multitude of people there, some buying, some selling. The murmur and hum of their voices and words could be heard more than a league off. Among us some soldiers who had been in different parts of the world, in Constantinople, all over Italy and in Rome, said that so large a market-place and so full of people, and so well-regulated and arranged, they had never beheld before.

Tlatelolco, an independent island city before its annexation by Tenochtitlan, was dominated by the 'tall and accursed temple' referred to above. More important in 1519, however, was the sacred precinct which lay at the heart of the Aztec capital and, by extension, the Aztec empire. In this paved *plaza* were combined the highest manifestations of religion and state. According to Spanish eyewitnesses, the precinct was enclosed by a *coatepantli* ('serpent wall') and four fortified gateways oriented to the cardinal directions. From the centre of the *plaza* rose the great double temple of Huitzilopochtli and Tláloc, god of rain and green growth. Recent archaeological excavations have shown that this colossal edifice, dedicated to warfare and agriculture, was formed in seven stages. Using vast amounts of earth infill, *tezontle* (volcanic rock) and lime, Aztec builders amplified the pyramidal structure by superimposing each new construction on the earlier ones. To mark its inauguration in 1487, twenty thousand captive warriors were sacrificed. Also located within the sacred precinct were monolithic stone sculptures and rows of trees, the *tzompantli* (skull-rack altar), priestly dwellings and monastery schools, arsenals guarded by soldiers, a ballcourt and several smaller temples.

There were temples, too, in the four administrative quarters of the capital, and in the many *calpulli* (wards) that made up each quarter. Roofs, noted Fray Juan de Torquemada, 'were of diverse and varied shapes . . . some of wood, and others of a straw like rye . . . beautifully worked, some being pyramidal, some square, some round, and some of other forms. And they made them so well that they did not seem to be of actual materials, but of very fine and delicate brushwork.' Walls were a brilliant mix of whiteness and colour. Using a technique admired by the *conquistadores*, city-dwellers rubbed stucco-faced buildings with smooth pebbles, burnishing them until they gleamed like silver or seemed 'made of jewels'.

Aztec society was highly stratified. The city's population was chiefly formed by the working or productive classes. Farmers and fishermen lived on the outskirts (see page 16). Carpenters, stone-cutters, masons, potters, metalsmiths and other artisans were located in the inner city, often in specially designated areas. Their single-storey houses were made of wood or adobe (sun-dried mud bricks). The artisans belonged to guilds and paid tribute to the emperor with their products. Some also gave their labour to public works, building temples, causeways, drainage systems or defensive barricades, as required by the state.

Religious, political, economic and social spheres were controlled by the Aztec élite. Tenochtitlan's imperial palaces and grand houses were situated near the sacred precinct. Built on two levels by skilled stonemasons, these incorporated interior courtyards filled with flowers and foliage. Some, according to Cortés, possessed 'very exquisite flower gardens both on the upper apartments as well as down below'. As Torquemada observed, the owners of these great houses 'were

In Tenochtitlan, only members of the élite were allowed to build on two levels. The Codex Florentino *(1564–65), compiled by Fray Bernardino de Sahagún, includes a survey of Aztec buildings in which houses of this type are described as 'sumptuous'. A similar two-storey residence is termed 'sturdy' and 'thick-walled'; foundations of stone and mortar are 'deep, well sunken into the earth'. Water from the flat roof was directed away from the walls by rainspouts.*

Illustration from the Codex Florentino *showing how city dwellings could be grouped together. In the example shown above, lintels and jambs are clearly of stone; here they appear to be made from wood.*

very solicitous to keep them very well whitewashed. . . . When part of the building, or some wall, lost its coating or became dull, it was immediately whitewashed and plastered again by officials in charge of this, who did nothing else nor served in any other capacity.' Rooms were 'very clean, polished, carpeted and tapestried with walls of cotton and feathers in many colours'. Some interior walls were decorated with vivid murals.

The *Conquistador Anónimo* ('Anonymous Conqueror') visited several 'very handsome and fine houses belonging to the chieftains, so large and with such offices, dwelling rooms, and gardens both above and below that they are wonderful to behold. I went more than four times to the emperor's residence, merely to look at it, and I always walked about until I was tired, yet I never managed to see the whole of it. It was the custom to have near the entrance of all the lords' houses very large halls and offices around a large patio, but in this house there was a hall so vast that it would easily hold more than three thousand persons, and it was so large that on the floor above [i.e., the roof] there was a terrace where thirty horsemen could have run a tilt as in a *plaza*.' The ruler and his retinue occupied apartments on the upper level; the ground floor housed courts of justice, arsenals, prisons and the public treasury. Also included within the palace grounds were workshops for weavers and artisans, a zoo, an aviary, a pond for aquatic birds, orchards, baths and luxuriant gardens.

The capital was sustained by trade and tribute. Luxury goods for the royal palace were obtained by the *pochteca* (merchants), who travelled in foreign territories. War, considered the most glorious of all activities, furnished captives for sacrifice and extended the boundaries of the Aztec empire. Subjugated nations paid taxes in finished goods and raw materials: these included vast quantities of maize, beans, cochineal, lime, *tezontle*, strong canes, copper axe-blades and wood. Every eighty days, according to the *Codex Mendoza*, one group of thirteen towns had jointly to provide 1,200 large wooden beams, 1,200 broad planks and 1,200 narrow planks.

Because theirs was the last civilization to evolve in pre-Conquest Mexico, the Aztec were able to draw on the cultural legacy of earlier peoples. The city of Teotihuacán (0–750) had adhered to a grand cosmic design, comprising massive pyramids, religious and civic edifices, *plazas*, wide avenues and residential complexes. Spatial relationships and the interplay of volumes were as important as architectural forms; religious symbolism dominated magnificent frescoes and sculptural friezes. The Toltec capital at Tula (700–1168) was primarily a ritual centre. Ceremonial buildings included colonnaded halls, ballcourts and a stepped pyramid crowned by a temple, its roof supported by colossal stone columns in the shape of warriors and plumed serpents. Tula's militarist culture was held in high regard by the Aztec, who took away sculptures and friezes for re-use in Tenochtitlan.

In pre-Hispanic Mexico furnishings were few. Here, Moctezuma II is seen addressing members of his council. They are seated on a petlatl *of palm or reeds. Mats of this type, which also served as beds, often featured elaborate designs. The emperor sits on his* icpalli, *or basketwork throne. According to the* Codex Florentino, *royal chairs were also made from cured leather or the skins of animals such as the ocelot and the wolf.*

Outside central Mexico, pre-Hispanic builders explored different styles. In the arid north, mud was shaped in large wooden moulds to form thick-walled agglomerations of dwellings on one or more levels. Surfaces were covered by a fine layer of mud, then painted in white, yellow and ochre. An ingenious system of channels brought fresh water into settlements, and carried away sewage water. At El Tajín (150–900), on the fertile Gulf Coast, buildings reflected the exuberance of nature. Stone façades, replete with scrollwork and bas-reliefs, were enlivened by the effects of light and shadow; structures were decorated in rich polychrome stucco. The Zapotec city of Monte Albán, founded *c.*200 BC on a hilltop in Oaxaca, reached the height of its power between 600 and 800. As at Teotihuacán, builders sought to combine architectural volume with vast, open spaces. Laid out around an immense *plaza* were pyramids, esplanades, courtyards, chambered structures, ballcourts and vaulted underground tombs adorned by mural paintings. As many as fifty thousand inhabitants may once have occupied houses on the terraces surrounding this great centre. After 800 this site was occupied by the Mixtec, who also left their mark on the Zapotec city of Mitla. Here, long masonry halls were arranged on platforms around the four sides of courtyards. Walls were intricately lined with geometric limestone mosaics. From descriptions of the colonial period, it is known that the spacious rooms of these palaces had flat roofs supported by huge horizontal beams of wood.

In the history of the New World, few peoples have matched the intellectual and artistic achievements of the Maya. Rooted in Olmec culture of the tenth century BC, this brilliant civilization reached its climax during the Classic period (300–900), then experienced a renaissance under central Mexican influence. Based on a loose federation of city states, Maya territories extended over nearly 324,000 square kilometres (125,000 sq. miles) from northwest Honduras, through the lowland forests of Campeche and the Guatemalan Petén region, to the open plains of Yucatán. The Maya devised complex calendrical systems and recorded their calculations with hieroglyphic inscriptions; they also excelled as muralists, sculptors, potters and architects. Materials for stonemasonry were abundant. Local limestone was burned to yield lime, and there were many deposits of gravel for use in mortar.

Although the ceremonial centres of the Maya differed in detail, they shared many features. Ranged around open spaces were stone stelae, masonry platforms, temple-pyramids, ballcourts and major edifices with carved lintels. Construction methods often relied on the corbelled vault. While interiors were dark and cramped, façades were variously embellished with stucco masks, relief panels and polychrome decoration. Buildings at Palenque were distinguished by elaborate roof combs. At Uxmal and neighbouring sites, edifices in Puuc style were faced with thin squares of limestone over a cement-and-rubble core, and

Opposite top *Nineteenth-century engraving showing the main façade of the Monjas (Nunnery) Annexe at the Maya site of Chichén Itzá, Yucatán. Built in Puuc style between the eighth and the early tenth centuries, it is faced with thin squares of limestone over a core of cement and rubble. Other characteristics include carved sky-serpent faces with long hook-shaped noses, frets and lattice-like designs.*

Transverse section of a Maya building with corbelled vaults, from Yucatán. Most Maya buildings stood on substructures; flat roofs were made of hard lime concrete. On the top, parallel with the front of the building, the high reticulated wall forms a decorative roof comb.

Right *Cross-sections of Maya corbelled vaults from the sites of Uaxactun, Palenque and Uxmal. Corbelling was a technique much used by the ancient Maya for roofing stone chambers. To achieve this effect, each course of stones had partially to over-sail the one beneath. Eventually the stones meet, or leave only a small gap, which can be spanned by a capstone. The earliest roof vaults were crudely constructed with rough, unshaped flat stones, laid in a thick bed of mortar and pebbles. Before the end of the Classic era the corbelled roof vault had gained acceptance throughout the lowland Maya area.*

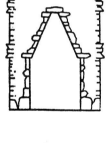

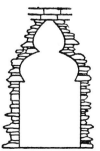

characterized by the exuberant use of stone mosaics on upper façades. When the Spaniards arrived, Maya culture had entered a period of decline; the *conquistadores* were nevertheless struck by the immensity of past achievements. 'If Yucatán were to gain a name and reputation', wrote Fray Diego de Landa in 1566, 'from the multitude, the grandeur and the beauty of its buildings, as other regions of the Indies have obtained by gold, silver and riches, its glory would spread like that of Peru and New Spain [Spanish Mexico].'

During the Classic period, most Maya lived in dispersed hamlets, cultivating the land and only resorting to the great religious centres during major ceremonies. Later came a shift to concentrated settlement. In the *Relación de las cosas de Yucatán*, Landa described Maya customs at the time of the Conquest: 'Before the Spaniards had conquered that country [Yucatán] the natives lived together in towns in a very civilized fashion. They kept the land well-cleared and free from weeds, and planted very good trees. Their dwelling-place was as follows – in the middle of the town were their temples with beautiful *plazas*, and all around the temples stood the houses of the lords and priests and then [those of] the most important people. Thus came the houses of the richest, and of those who were held in the highest estimation nearest to these, and at the outskirts of the town were the houses of the lowest class.'

Today the peninsular Maya habitually raise their homes on low platforms to avoid flooding; rectangular mounds of earth and stone at many archaeological sites show that this practice is ancient. At Uxmal and other centres, continuity is confirmed by stylized representations of domestic dwellings in façade decorations and wall paintings; modern houses resemble them closely (see ills 7 and 45). In his account of Maya life, Landa offered the following information about house construction and distribution of space:

In building their houses their method was to cover them with an excellent [grass] thatch which they have in abundance, or with the leaves of a palm well adapted to that purpose, the roof being very steep to prevent its raining through. They then run a wall lengthways of the whole house, leaving certain doorways into the half which they call the back of the house, where they have their beds. The other half they whiten with a fine whitewash, and the chiefs also have beautiful frescoes there. This part serves for the reception and the lodging of guests, and has no doorway but is open along the whole length of the house. The roof drops very low in front as a protection against sun and rain; also, they say, the better to defend the interior from enemies in case of necessity.

The common people build the chiefs' dwellings at their own expense. The houses having no doors, it is held a grave offence to do any wrong to another's house; in the back, however, they have a small door for household uses. They sleep on beds made of small rods, covered with mats, and with their mantles of cotton as covering. In the summer they sleep in the front part of the house on the mats, especially the men. Away from the house the entire village sows the fields of the chief, cares for them, and harvests what is required for him and his household; and whenever they hunt and fish, or at the salt gathering time, they always give a part to the chief; in these matters everything is always in common.

Most chronicles of the Conquest period focused on grandiose architecture in an urban setting. Far less attention was paid to modest rural dwellings, which were generally made from perishable materials. The *Relación de Michoacán*, however, compiled between 1539 and 1541 by a Franciscan friar, recounted the history of the Purépecha, or Tarascos, who inhabit western Mexico and were never conquered by the Aztec. Although the manuscript includes few references to architecture, it is accompanied by forty-four illustrations by an Indian artist. Many show the houses of ordinary people. While some were square or rectangular, others were apparently round; roofs were thatched. Sixteenth-century reports for the state of Oaxaca incorporated brief descriptions of local buildings. Mixtec dwellings were small and irregularly dispersed among maize fields. In Tilantongo, for example, 'The edifices and houses of the natives resemble cells: they are made from *terrado* [earth overlay used on flat roofs] and adobe and white stone; they stand a fair distance from one another because houses and cultivation plots are situated together; they build with stones, wooden beams, planks, lime.'

Illustrations from the Relación de Michoacán *(1539–41). Below* Thatched dwelling. *Contemporary houses in the state of Michoacán often have a covered porch where people can work and rest (see page 45; also ill. 28). Below right* Round dwelling with a thatched roof; the inverted pot prevented rain from entering at the apex. *In the* Relación de Michoacán *this house illustrates a section entitled 'The manner of marriage among the lower-class people'. Houses of similar design are found today in Oaxaca and other regions (see page 62, top).*

The *Historia general de las cosas de Nueva España* (*c*.1540–77) remains one of the most thorough studies of indigenous life ever undertaken in Mexico. Compiled with the help of Indian informants by Fray Bernardino de Sahagún, it documents Aztec beliefs and customs. The accompanying illustrations are referred to separately as the *Codex Florentino*. In the architectural section, Sahagún considers a range of modest, one-storey dwellings. Although most are square or rectangular, he includes 'cylindrical' houses with pointed roofs of thatch. Flat-roofed houses incorporated beams covered by planks 'with earth above' (see page 23). Walls were made from planks, poles, sticks, adobe or stone; surfaces could be whitened or painted. Reed or grass huts were 'mud-plastered, with chinks filled'. In the middle of each house three stones formed a hearth; interiors were dark, and furnishings sparse. Then, as now, dwellings were bordered by small plots of land where inhabitants could work and rest.

The lives of neighbouring peoples were also discussed in the *Historia general*. The Otomí, for example, 'provided themselves with huts of straw or grass; they did not greatly esteem flat-roofed houses'. In the north, however, the Teochichimeca 'had their homes nowhere . . . they lived in the forests, the grassy plains, the deserts, among the crags'; their ruler's palace was 'perhaps a grass house, or only a straw hut or a cave in the cliffs'.

Aztec and Mixtec codices, painted around the time of the Conquest, add to our knowledge of domestic and ritual practices. Mention has already been made of the *Codex Mendoza*: while Part II was a copy of Moctezuma's tribute roll, Part III depicted the 'life from year to year' of the Aztec. Also helpful for our understanding are small archaeological replicas of houses and temples. Made of stone or pottery, these have been found in several regions. In Nayarit, the dead were buried with hand-modelled dwellings of painted pottery. Arranged on one or two levels with outside stairways, these diminutive habitations for the afterlife incorporated dogs, birds and human figures engaged in everyday activities.

In 1519 the Aztec held the balance of power in Middle America; by 1521 their vast empire had fallen. Well served by their metal weapons, gunpowder and horses, Cortés and his followers were assisted in their conquest by the Tlaxcalans, who had long been rivals of the Aztec, and by subjugated peoples eager to free themselves from Aztec oppression. Moctezuma, unnerved by a series of

Above left Simple Aztec shelter, with straw roof. Similar constructions are widely used today on agricultural land. Centre Aztec house with plank walls and four-sided thatched roof of grass or straw. Right Dwelling with wooden roof. The shingled roofs shown on page 70 (ill. 29) have a similar appearance. Walls could also be of masonry.

Round Mixtec building of straw from Oaxaca, portrayed in stylized fashion in the Codex Zouche-Nuttall (c. 1300–1500). Bundles of stalks were anchored to horizontal rods, then positioned in overlapping layers. (For a contemporary example of this same technique, see ill. 20.)

seemingly threatening portents, allowed the adventurers into his capital. Later, he was taken prisoner and forced to declare himself a vassal of the king of Spain. In the summer of 1521 the Spaniards besieged Tenochtitlan. Cut off from food supplies and beset by smallpox, the inhabitants watched their great city crumble around them. An anonymous Náhuatl poem records this final assault:

> . . . Our spears lie broken in the streets
> Our hair is torn
> Gone are the roofs of our houses
> Their walls red with blood
> Worms crawl across the streets and squares
> Brains cling to the walls
> Red is the water, lurid as dye,
> When we drink it tastes of sulphur.

Many contradictions underlay colonial rule in New Spain (Spanish Mexico). Based on private enterprise, the Conquest was won by brave and ambitious men who sought a rich reward. The Spanish Crown also required its portion of all revenues, officially termed the Royal Fifth. Eight hundred years of Moorish occupation had accustomed the Spaniards to an economy largely based on booty wrested from their 'pagan' enemies. With the Moors driven out, Spain was free to deploy her military powers in the New World and to secure for herself an alternative source of wealth. Charles V was not only king of Spain, however. As emperor of the Holy Roman Empire, it was his moral duty to justify military

The Old World meets the New: Hernán Cortés is welcomed by the people of Tlaxcala. In this scene from the Lienzo de Tlaxcala, *he sits in the Tlaxcalan palace with doña Marina, his Indian interpreter and mistress; ranged behind are the soldiers of the Spanish army. Cortés is being greeted by Maxixcatzin, one of the four lords of Tlaxcala. The visitors and their horses are accompanied by gifts of food.*

conquest in terms of religious conversion. The colonists saw themselves as Catholic crusaders, obliged to 'extend the knowledge, cult and splendour' of the faith, while controlling Indian labour and production. Inevitably, Christian ideals clashed with greed. 'Once across the sea', the Franciscan Gerónimo de Mendieta commented scathingly, 'the pettiest Spaniard thinks himself the greatest gentleman . . . there is not a man among them, no matter how lowly, who will touch a hoe or a plough.'

Before the Conquest, 371 towns had paid tribute to Tenochtitlan. From Aztec tribute rolls the Spaniards acquired valuable knowledge of the population and economy of newly won territories. The institution of *encomienda* (from *encomendar*, 'to entrust') consigned groups of Indians to privileged Spanish settlers, who commanded their labour and exacted tribute in return for religious instruction. In practice, this system was open to widespread abuse: on newly formed estates, many unscrupulous *encomenderos* (grantees) worked their charges to exhaustion. Vast fortunes accrued, founded on the export of gold, silver, cochineal, indigo, balsam, vanilla and other native resources, while the introduction of European cereals and cattle generated additional wealth for Spanish landholders.

The *Memorial of the Indians of Tepetlaoztoc* (*c*.1555) offers a rare insight into rural exploitation. Through words and pictures, it recounts a lawsuit between local Indians and Juan Velásquez de Salazar, the absentee *encomendero*; goods and services, provided between 1522 and 1554, are duly recorded. In addition to their usual tribute, which included fine woven mantles, decorated blouses and skirts, the Indians had been compelled by two successive *mayordomos* (estate stewards) to build without recompense a two-storey house and a large water mill. Those who failed to comply were cruelly punished: many Indians died, while others took flight. The Spanish judge and the government official ruled in favour of the Indians. They ordered the *encomendero* to pay them compensation, and set the level of future tribute.

Towards the end of the century the place of the *encomienda* was largely taken by *repartimiento* – a system of forced but paid labour. With the implementation of stricter controls, extreme forms of exploitation were prohibited, yet the lot of most Indians remained wretched. Crop failures and imported diseases posed another threat. In 1521 the colony had a native population of approximately ten million; by 1550 it had dropped to around five million. 'Without being entirely finished off, how can the Indians, being so few and every day fewer, keep on serving and supporting the Spaniards, every day more?', asked Fray Mendieta. By the turn of the century, an estimated two million Indians were left.

Gerónimo de Mendieta and other Mendicant friars campaigned tirelessly on the Indians' behalf. In their desire to save souls, they eradicated native forms of worship, yet they opposed the widely held view that Indians, as unreasoning and

Agriculture was essential for the sustenance of the colony. As encomiendas *declined in importance, individuals with capital were increasingly permitted to purchase land. This 1764 plan showed the* hacienda *(large rural estate) of San Juan de los Otates near León, Guanajuato. A fortified wall surrounded the grounds: here, the workforce lived in tiny, scattered dwellings. The* casco *(main house and administrative centre) was square: a single entrance safeguarded the security of inhabitants. Rooms enclosed an interior patio with trees and plants. Three doorways and an archway gave access to the patio; four windows admitted light and air. The chapel is situated on one corner of the house. During the eighteenth century most wealthy families owned one or more* haciendas. *With the passing of time, earlier buildings were enlarged or rebuilt to meet changing needs. (The plan of a late nineteenth-century* hacienda *appears on page 31.)*

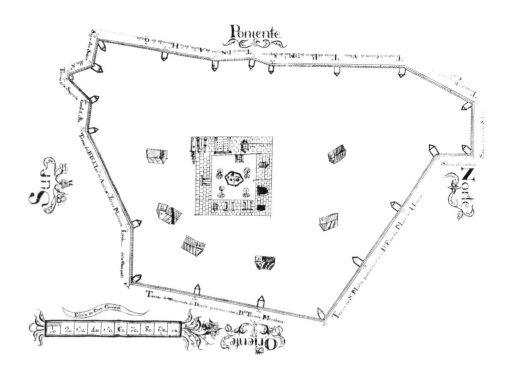

inferior beings, were fit only to be the slaves of Spaniards. 'How can anyone call them irrational or beasts?', asked one group of Franciscans in a letter to the emperor dated 1533. 'How can they be held incapable, with such sumptuousness in their buildings, such subtle exquisiteness in their handiwork, and when they are such notable silversmiths and painters. . . ?'.

The Mendicants served as a stabilizing force throughout New Spain. They were also the most prolific builders of the sixteenth century. In territories allotted exclusively to each order, Franciscans, Dominicans and Augustinians founded some four hundred monastery towns, supervising the construction by Indian labourers of ecclesiastical buildings, aqueducts, schools and hospitals. For many of their earliest undertakings, the friars made use of native methods and materials. At Maní in Yucatán, two hundred Indians built a Franciscan church and

Sixteenth-century drawing by an Indian artist of the open chapel at Jilotepec in the state of Mexico. Such constructions had no precedent in Europe. During this period of mass-conversion, churches could not always accommodate vast Indian gatherings. Open chapels, situated inside the walled atrium of the church, enabled priests to officiate in view of the congregation.

monastery in a single day, using light wood and no nails. Fray Toribio de Benavente, known as Motolinía, praised those who 'put no spike or nail in their buildings, which do not lack strength because of that'. In Jalisco, Michoacán and the Huasteca, provisional monasteries were often of adobe. (Although sun-dried mud blocks had long been used in southern Spain, they were a novelty for some Spaniards.) *Tapial* (rammed earth) was also employed in the making of walls. As in pre-Conquest times, builders would pack earth, mud, rubble and straw into large wooden frames; these remained in place while the mixture hardened.

Few traces remain today of such makeshift constructions, replaced in later decades by durable masonry. Unlike the country houses of most *encomenderos*, who preferred town life and hoped to retire with their riches to Spain, these fortress-like structures of stone were built to last. With their heavily buttressed walls, the monasteries of Acolman, Actopan, Huaquechula, Huejotzingo and Yecapixtla – to name but a few – endure as mighty monuments to the religious conviction and inventive powers of the crusading friars. Largely untrained in the art of building, they drew on their memories of Old World architecture, and sought inspiration in European engravings and dissertations. Numerous edicts offered guidance. In their chapter of 1569, Franciscans were told that buildings should be 'plain, strong and without any novelty'. In practice, however, the friars had considerable freedom. Most monasteries were similar in plan and general design, yet ornamental detail was rarely standardized. Far from Spain, in an alien climate and an alien land, Gothic, romanesque, Renaissance and Plateresque styles were interpreted and modified. *Mudéjar* (art made for Spanish Christians in a Moslem or Moslem-influenced manner) also left its mark in Mexico. Favoured *mudéjar* elements included pyramidal and stepped merlons, doorways enclosed in rectangular *alfiz* mouldings, polylobed or scalloped arches, *alfarje* or *artesonado* wooden ceilings, areas of dense patterning on façades, and painted decorations repeated on walls, ceilings and vaults.

The New World metamorphosis of Old World styles was due in large part to the sensibility of Indian builders. Monastery schools gave instruction in carpentry, masonry, painting, carving, metalworking and other European skills. As Fray Mendieta noted appreciatively *c.*1580, 'Almost all the good and notable handiwork here in the Indies (at least in New Spain) is done by the Indians, because the Spaniards, masters of many crafts, rarely do more than give the work to the Indians, and tell them how they want it done. And they do it so well, no one could do it better.' With an aptitude and speed that astonished the friars, Indian craftsmen applied new techniques and adapted old ones. Bishop Zumárraga wrote in praise of thirteen master-craftsmen, who learned in two years to carve Spanish saints worthy of his cathedral. Motolinía boasted that by 1540 'great painters have arisen . . . since samples and images have been brought by the Spaniards from Flanders and Italy, there is neither image nor *retablo*, no

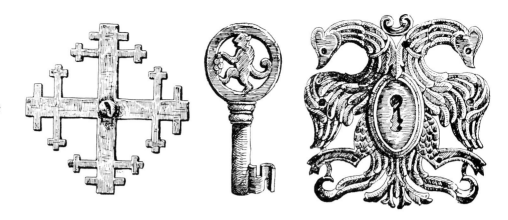

matter how excellent, which they do not imitate well.' The Indians did more than carry out instructions, however. In their carvings and love of ornamental detail, they revealed an aesthetic vitality that was altogether their own. This intermingling on Mexican soil of European and Indian styles is referred to by art historians as *tequitqui*.

Austere living conditions in the rural monasteries contrasted sharply with mores in the capital, where a keen appetite for luxury accompanied new-found affluence. Built on the ruins of Tenochtitlan, the Spanish metropolis was described as 'already very beautiful' by Cortés, within months of his victory, in a letter to Charles V. 'So well and so quickly does the work go', he wrote just three years later, '. . . that many of the houses are already finished, and others are well on their way. There is such a plenty of stone, lime, wood, and bricks which the natives make, that the houses are mostly large and comely. Your Sacred Majesty may be certain that within five years this will be the noblest and most populous city in the world, and one of the best built.'

When initiating his ambitious programme of reconstruction, Cortés recruited those Indian warriors who had helped him to destroy the city. Later, labour was obtained through *encomienda* and *repartimiento*. Squared stones, wooden beams and rubble from Aztec edifices were re-used for grand houses, government buildings, fortifications and churches. The prodigious efforts of those early years, when 'more people were busy in the work than in the building of the Temple of Jerusalem', were evoked by Motolinía: 'They carry everything on their backs; they drag the beams and heavy stones along the ground with ropes; and since their numbers had to make up for lack of ingenuity, the stone or beam that called for a hundred men was moved by four hundred.' 'So many were working on the buildings . . . that a man could hardly pick his way through the streets. . . . Many were killed by falling beams or by falling from a height; others lost their life under buildings they were taking down in one place to put up in another, especially when they dismantled the chief temples of the Devil . . .'.

As in country areas, Indian builders were taught to use new materials and skills. Although fired bricks had been deployed at several pre-Hispanic sites, their widespread use – together with that of terracotta roof tiles – dates from the Conquest. The European method of vaulting, first demonstrated in 1525, caused considerable alarm. According to Motolinía, the chancel of the church of San

Francisco had a vault made by a mason from Castile. 'The Indians were greatly astonished to see something vaulted, and could only suppose that when the supporting scaffold was taken away, everything would surely fall down.'

Trained architects were in short supply. The city's overall plan was entrusted by Cortés to Alonso García Bravo, a soldier-*conquistador* and 'a very good geometer' (surveyor). The Aztec precinct was converted into a new *plaza*: paved with smooth stones from the old courtyard, it incorporated religious and civic buildings, and *portales* (arcades) for the merchants. The great market place at Tlatelolco was also rebuilt with long colonnades. The main avenues, which led from the precinct to the causeways and the lake, were retained in García Bravo's checkerboard design. Streets were regularly swept and flushed.

In the *traza* (the grid-like residential zone) and on the old Aztec street of Tacuba, Spanish *encomenderos* erected fortress-like palaces with battlemented tops, corner towers and escutcheons over the portals. Although some edifices were of stuccoed brick, sixteenth-century edicts demanded façades of stone, straight and flush with neighbouring buildings. The most powerful *encomendero* was Hernán Cortés, now marqués del Valle de Oaxaca. Granted 22 towns by Charles V, he could command the labour and tribute of 23,000 Indian vassals. In keeping with his exalted status, Cortés chose to remodel Moctezuma's palace on the east side of the *plaza* and a second royal palace on the west side. In later years the latter passed to his son and heir, while the former became the viceregal residence. There were few changes, meanwhile, in the domestic architecture of the native workforce. As the century advanced, increasing numbers of Indians settled at the city's edges. Their houses and *chinampas*, set out in traditional manner, remained outside the Spanish plan.

In the provinces, other settlements rose to prominence. Modelled on the capital, these included Guadalajara, Pátzcuaro, Oaxaca City (also planned by Alonso García Bravo), Tlaxcala City and Puebla de los Angeles. In the Maya region of Yucatán, the city of Mérida was built with masonry from local pyramids. Strict rules governed urban development (see page 97). Although building ordinances would later arrive from Spain, guidelines were established by Cortés in 1525: 'After felling the trees you must begin to clear the site, and then, following the plan I have made, you must mark out the public places just as they are shown: the *plaza*, church, town hall and jail, market and slaughterhouse, hospital. . . . Then you will indicate to each citizen his particular lot, as shown on the plan, and do the same for those who come later. You will make sure the streets are very straight, and accordingly will find people who know how to lay them out.'

Rising prosperity and an influx of settlers led to the capital's continued expansion. In 1565 the Philippines came under Spanish rule. With New Spain as the transit point between Europe and the Orient, wealthy citizens could buy

The Mexico City Cathedral before reconstruction in 1585. Built in the new Spanish plaza *by Indian labourers soon after the Conquest, it incorporated stones from the great Aztec pyramid of Tláloc and Huitzilopochtli. After the late 1520s, bells were regularly cast in the capital. When not hung in church towers, they were often positioned in* espadañas *(arch-pierced bell screens). Here, the* espadaña *crowns the façade.*

Aztec house-builders from the Codex Florentino, *shown roofing a house with earth. This ancient form of domestic architecture is still found in modern Mexico (see ill. 24). Today, roofs often incorporate a layer of earth mixed with sand and lime (see ill. 17). Builders in Tenochtitlan worked with copper implements; iron and steel tools were introduced by Spanish settlers.*

Baroque styles of architecture took effect during the early seventeenth century and lasted in general until the closing years of the eighteenth. The Cathedral in Chihuahua City (1717–89) has a handsome dome and twin towers that rise in three diminishing storeys of columns and arches. The profusely ornamented façade is adorned with statues placed in niches between twisted Salomonic columns.

porcelain, ivory, silks and other luxury goods. Gradually, streets were paved and canals filled in. Flowering trees and gardens were introduced. Guilds, closed initially to Indians, controlled standards of craftsmanship and materials. Earlier building defects were remedied, and edifices remodelled. Progress was hampered, however, by the marshy terrain and by the flooding that followed deforestation. The rebuilding campaign had denuded the surrounding hills of cedar, cypress and pine trees. Now, topsoil was being washed down into the lakes. As heavy buildings listed or sank, constant repairs were needed: new floors were laid, pillars and doorways elevated. Yet, despite these problems, the city grew in splendour while its formal order, related still to the Aztec plan, became ever clearer. By 1574, there were approximately fifteen thousand Spaniards in the capital, and large numbers of Indians, blacks, mulattoes and *mestizos* (Mexicans of mixed European and Indian descent). Fray Alonso Ponce, who saw the city in 1585, praised the 'very good houses and handsome streets, broad and long, which appear to have been made from the same mould since they are so equal and alike'. Samuel de Champlain, a Frenchman who visited in 1599, found the streets 'extremely well laid out', and the city 'superbly constructed of splendid churches, palaces and fine houses'. Today, few sixteenth-century examples of civil architecture remain. When not demolished by later generations, buildings were modified to suit prevailing tastes.

The vogue for Baroque architecture, painting and decoration was apparent in Mexico from the early decades of the seventeenth century. The style was introduced from Spain and enthusiastically adopted by the *criollos* (Mexican-born Spaniards). Alienated from a mother country that few had visited, and regarded as inferior by the *peninsulares* (Spaniards born in Spain), the *criollos* formed an increasingly large and wealthy group. By 1750 Baroque fashions had become ultra-Baroque. Laden with ornamentation, ecclesiastical and secular buildings were unequivocally and exuberantly Mexican. Some constructions, completed over long periods of time, displayed a blend of traits, combining the simpler outlines of earlier decades with the riotous embellishment of later phases. Meanwhile, in country districts, local craftsmen drew inspiration from urban architecture. Their vivid and imaginative creations are often termed *barroco popular*.

Thomas Gage, a Dominican friar from England, visited New Spain in 1625. His memoirs, written after conversion to radical Protestantism, evoked the 'vain ostentation' of the Spanish colony. Spectacular riches, displayed in the capital's churches, were 'infinite in price and value' (see page 159). In fashionable areas of the city, the trappings of wealth were boldly flaunted. Men and women were 'excessive in their apparel, using more silks than stuffs and cloth'. Coaches exceeded 'in cost the best of the Court of Madrid', while many horses had 'bridles and shoes of silver'. The Alameda Park, laid out in 1593, was an important meeting place for the élite. To 'this pleasant shady field . . . full of trees and walks' there came each afternoon, at 'about four of the clock', some 'two thousand coaches, full of gallants, ladies and citizens, to see and to be seen, to court and to be courted'. Indians lived 'in the suburbs of the city', but their lands were prey to the city's expansion. Each day, according to Gage, Spaniards would 'cozen them of the small plot of ground where their houses stand': 'of three or four houses of Indians, they build up one good and fair . . . with gardens and orchards. And so is almost all Mexico new built with very fair and spacious houses with gardens of recreation.'

Later observers included Francisco de Ajofrín, a Capuchin friar who visited New Spain in 1763. Impressed by the glories of the capital, he also noted the effects of social inequality: 'Although in Mexico [City] there are great things, illustrious gentlemen, wealthy people, vehicles, carriages, finery and everything in profusion, yet the common peoples are so numerous, so ragged and tattered, that they disfigure and sully everything, dismaying those who have recently arrived from Europe . . . in this city are seen two diametrically opposed extremes: much wealth and maximum poverty; many fine costumes and extreme nudity; great cleanliness and great filth.'

During the eighteenth century many seignorial residences were remodelled, while others were newly built (see pages 162–5). All enclosed at least one patio. At street level, in the main patio, small businesses would sometimes operate: if these were not family-owned, the householder charged rent. Large mansions often had an *entresuelo*, equivalent to the contemporary mezzanine, where visitors were lodged. The *entresuelo* also provided storage space for merchandise or the produce from country estates. An imposing stairway led to the highest level: as the driest and the healthiest, it was occupied by members of the immediate family. A *corredor* overlooked the main patio and gave access to the various rooms. The drawing room was situated at the front of the house; wealthy families also had a music room, a dining room, a chapel and several reception rooms. Horses and carriages were kept in the back patio. The servants' quarters were reached by a second, more modest, stairway. Roofs were flat, so inhabitants could stroll or sit under canopies and enjoy the view. These same living arrangements were maintained by wealthy citizens throughout the greater part of

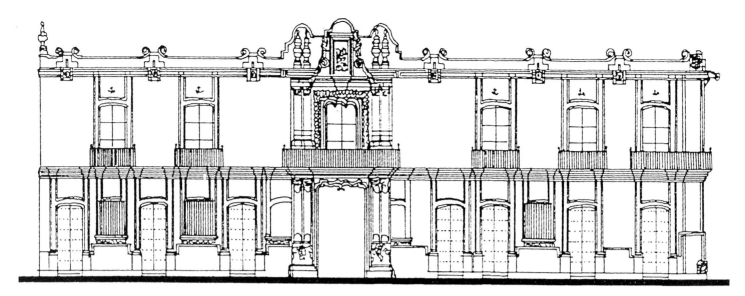

Palatial residence of the Condes de Santiago de Calimaya in Mexico City. Originally built during the sixteenth century, it incorporates a carved pre-Hispanic serpent's head at one corner. In 1779 the building was extensively remodelled in Baroque style by the Mexican architect Francisco Guerrero y Torres. The entrance of carved stonework is exceptionally rich: engaged Ionic columns support an entablature with elaborate dentils; an arch frames the doorway. The wooden door (not seen here) was carved in the Philippines to a Mexican design. Jambs are carried up to the cornice. Carved stone waterspouts take the form of cannons. The central patio is bordered by columns; the fountain, decorated with a two-tailed mermaid, is shown on page 164 (ill. 238).

the nineteenth century (see page 160). Lavish exteriors incorporated monumental entrances. Façades, often of reddish *tezontle*, displayed intricate carvings in grey-white sandstone. Other features included corner towers, statues in niches, balconies with wrought ironwork, massive wooden doors surmounted by coats of arms, gargoyles and ornate friezes. Door and window jambs were extended upwards. Windows to the street were masked in Moorish style by decorative iron grillework.

Unusually for Mexico City, the residence of the Condes del Valle de Orizaba was faced with blue-and-white *azulejos* (glazed tiles). Puebla de los Angeles, however, could be described as the 'city of tiles'. Introduced by Spanish settlers, the art of tin-glazing gave rise also to richly patterned earthenware jars and fine tableware. Referred to as *Talavera*, because it resembled pottery from Talavera de la Reina in Spain, output combined Islamic, Spanish, Italian, Chinese and indigenous design elements. During the full flowering of Mexican Baroque, brick walls, church domes and fountains were resplendent with gleaming, polychrome tiles; so too were the kitchens, halls and stairways of private houses. Stucco-encrusted façades were another feature of Poblano architecture. One mansion, replete with delicate, icing-like embellishments, is aptly known as La Casa del Alfeñique ('Sugar-Paste House'). In the city, but more especially in country towns such as Santa María Tonanzintla, church interiors exhibited a profusion of plaster figures: brilliant with gold leaf and colour, clusters of angels, saints, cherubs, animals, flowers and fruit covered walls and ceilings.

Baroque exuberance retained its appeal throughout much of New Spain. In the capital, however, building styles after 1785 were dominated by neo-classicism and regulated by the newly formed Royal Academy of San Carlos. During this period of artistic severity and European rationalism, academicians such as Manuel Tolsá (the Spanish architect) expounded Greco-Roman ideals of 'good taste' and 'noble simplicity'. Because Baroque styles were rejected as 'confused' and 'arbitrary', many church interiors were stripped of decoration. In 1792 a decree was issued by the Mexico City police: henceforth, only Academy-

In Mexico City, the Gran Teatro de Santa Anna, later renamed the Gran Teatro Nacional, was designed in imposing neo-classical style by the Spanish architect Lorenzo de la Hidalga (1810–72). Inaugurated in 1844, it was subsequently demolished. The façade was partially screened by massive free-standing columns that supported the entablature of the portico. During the 1841–44 presidency of Santa Anna, theatre and opera companies from Italy, France and Spain were invited to perform in the capital.

approved projects would be permitted in the capital. Predictably, most buildings of this date were for government use. Tolsá's Colegio de Minería (Mining College) is neo-classicism at its grandest: built at great cost between 1797 and 1813, it has 238 rooms, 13 stairways, 11 fountains and 7 patios.

In 1821 the Wars for Independence brought an end to Spanish rule, but failed to weaken European influence. New Spain was renamed Mexico in memory of the Mexica (Aztec), yet the spirit of neo-classicism still prevailed. Despite political upheavals, foreign interventions and chronic economic crisis, the Academy still sought to dictate architectural policy: existing buildings were remodelled and war damage was made good, although new projects were few. Beset by problems, the capital remained a world unto itself, peopled by the richest and the poorest in the land. Frances Calderón de la Barca, the Scottish wife of the Foreign Minister for Spain, was a witness in the early 1840s to 'the melancholy effects produced by years of civil war and unsettled government'. Her letters tell of revolts, ceasefires and government proclamations. They also evoke church festivals and grand processions, visits to the theatre and the opera, excursions in costly carriages imported from England, bullfights and glittering balls – including an English ball at Tolsá's 'magnificent Minería'. De la Barca described the interiors of palatial residences (see page 160), praised the Academy for the 'simple and noble taste which distinguishes the Mexican buildings', and lamented the absence of a Mexican middle class.

By 1858, when Carl Sartorius published his book *Mexico, Landscapes and Popular Sketches*, white-collar workers and small independent entrepreneurs had begun to fill this gap. Far from prosperous yet possessed of 'a tolerable income', they lived in conditions that were comfortable though rudimentary: 'The floor of the whole house is paved with flags, carefully cemented. In the saloon and some of the rooms, the flags are painted so as to resemble mosaic. The walls are unpapered, plastered, and painted with arabesques; the ceiling is the same.' Round the rim of most cities, a vast underclass lived in 'mean and dirty' suburbs. Here, Sartorius found adobe houses, lean and hungry dogs, poverty and dirt. 'The wealthy Creole', meanwhile, was 'a friend to luxury', with 'showy equipages' and 'numerous servants'. This observer, like Ajofrín before him, noted 'splendour and luxury on the one hand, filth and nakedness on the other'.

During the brief reign of Archduke Maximilian of Austria, emperor of Mexico between 1864 and 1867, French influence intensified. Aristocratic homes boasted imported pianos and carpets, crystal chandeliers, rosewood furniture, fine paintings, delicate porcelain and French bathroom fittings. In summer, the wealthy withdrew from the capital to country estates or to newly built villas in the outlying districts of Tacubaya, Coyoacán and Tacuba. The preference for foreign fashions reached its apogee under Porfirio Díaz, however. After 1876, political stability and increasing industrialization brought sustained economic growth, attracting foreign investment and foreign settlers. In Mexico City elegant shops, theatres, cafés and restaurants catered for the needs of the old élite and the new bourgeoisie. Magnificent balls and dinners were held at the Casino Español (see page 169), the Jockey Club (located in the erstwhile palace of the Condes del Valle de Orizaba), the Tívoli and the Club Alemán. In an effort to bolster the country's own self-respect and its image abroad, Díaz embarked on a campaign of building and renovation. Broad tree-lined avenues were created in the capital, while problems of drainage and flooding were resolved by British engineers. Telephones and electric lighting became widespread during the 1880s; trams and cars were introduced in 1901 and 1904 respectively.

During this time of positivism and 'progress', colonial dwellings were abandoned by the wealthy in favour of modern residences in new *colonias* (fashionable neighbourhoods). With growing freedom, Mexican and non-Mexican

The vogue for European fashions continued throughout the nineteenth century. Furniture of this type and household items such as dinner services, glassware and linen were imported for use in wealthy town residences and haciendas.

architects combined Gothic, Renaissance, Romanesque, Plateresque, Moorish, Baroque, Rococo, neo-classical and, eventually, Art Nouveau styles (see pages 158, 166–7 and 170–1). Behind richly ornamented façades, rooms, gardens and patios were distributed in an increasingly European manner. In the field of public architecture, interest in recent archaeological discoveries led in some cases to the incorporation of pre-Hispanic features. Developments in the technology of cast iron were also influential (see ill. 246). Outside the capital, in provincial streets and *plazas*, government spending was responsible for handsome cast-iron lamps and benches, monuments and bandstands (see ills. 143, 145 and 245). Whereas neo-classicism had attracted few devotees, the Porfirian emphasis on decoration had popular appeal. In centres such as Jerez, Mérida and Ciudad del Carmen, local buildings reflected the eclecticism of contemporary tastes (see pages 47, top, and 52).

Porfirian fashions and rising prosperity also left their mark on Mexico's *haciendas*, or country estates. The Díaz régime promoted large-scale landholdings. Although the 1910 census listed 8,245 *haciendas*, wealthy families often owned 15 or more. By the early twentieth century, in the state of Chihuahua, Luis Terrazas had accumulated approximately 50 *haciendas* and smaller ranches, totalling over 3 million hectares (7 million acres). (His daughter married her first

Architectural project conceived in 1898 by Emilio Dondé for a family dwelling in Mexico City. Sustained economic growth during the Porfirian era (1876–1911) fostered the rise of the middle class and the creation of new residential areas in the capital.

Porfirio Díaz (1830–1915), before his second marriage. When this photograph was taken, c. 1881, don Porfirio (seated on the right) was about 51 years old; his bride-to-be, Carmen Romero Rubio (standing, centre) was 18. Born to a family of modest means in the city of Oaxaca, Díaz was to control the destiny of the Mexican nation for a third of a century. Determined to eradicate chaos and to attract foreign investors, he espoused the positivist dictum of Order and Progress. His administration brought a rapid rise in manufacturing; improved harbour and dock facilities; implemented the growth of the railways; regenerated the mining industry and reduced banditry. This Pax Porfiriana was protected by increasingly authoritarian and brutal measures, however, while the costs of modernization were borne by the rural peasantry and the urban poor.

The hacienda of Tepenacasco, near Tulancingo, Hidalgo, c. 1881. The imposing espadaña (arch-pierced bell screen) is a feature of many haciendas. The inscription over the entrance reads, 'In this refinement and solitude I enjoy the treasure of peace'.

cousin, Enrique Creel, whose own *haciendas* covered more than 690,000 hectares [1,700,000 acres].) Some estates encompassed several operations, but most derived their income from a single source (see page 132). The ecology of many regions had been transformed during the colonial period by the introduction of cattle, and crops such as wheat and sugarcane. In Yucatán, however, *hacendados* (*hacienda*-owners) acquired riches through the cultivation of *henequén*, or sisal, while the states of Mexico, Hidalgo and Tlaxcala favoured the production of *pulque* (see pages 154–5). As in pre-Hispanic times, this intoxicating drink is made by fermenting the sweet sap of the *maguey* plant. Frances Calderón de la Barca was one of many observers to marvel at the 'mighty maguey plant, the American agave, which will flourish on the most arid soil'. It was, she noted, 'a source of unfailing profit . . . so that many of the richest families in the capital owe their fortune entirely to the produce of their magueys'. Each day, under Porfirio Díaz, special trains carried *pulque* from the Apan region to the capital, where it was sold in *pulquerías*.

On many *haciendas*, existing buildings were enlarged and remodelled to meet changing needs. On others, great houses were newly built to emulate European castles or English stately homes. Gothic pointed arches, medieval battlements and Moorish minarets were transposed to Mexican landscapes of agaves and prickly pears. Luxuriant gardens, plant-filled patios, painted scenes on walls and ceilings, tiles from England and statues from Paris were complemented by costly furnishings (see pages 50–1). Outbuildings were suited to their different functions (see pages 50, 148–53, 180–3). *Hacendados* rarely lived on their estates; usually they made brief visits, leaving administrators in charge of production.

Visitors to Mexico during the *Porfiriato* left evocative accounts of *hacienda* life. 'The Lord of the *hacienda* is "de facto", if not "de jure" lord of his labourers,' noted Thomas Unett Brocklehurst in 1881. His book, *Mexico To-Day: A Country with a Great Future . . .*, included a detailed description of

Tepenacasco, an 18,000-hectare (40,000-acre) estate in the state of Hidalgo. Between four and five hundred people worked for the Tejira family; although various crops were grown for local consumption, cattle and dairy produce constituted the main source of revenue. Water for irrigation was collected in 'ten large dams, or reservoirs'; there was also 'the lake Zupitlan, formed by a wall embankment a mile in length, and shared in by two neighbouring haciendas.' When in residence, the owners lived comfortably:

> The house is a large one-storied building with two inner courts. On two blank walls of the principal court, round which there ran a handsome corridor, are two large fresco paintings, one representing St. James Palace with the guards in the dress of George the Third, the other was easily recognised as the garden front of Old Eaton Hall, Cheshire. The outer court had a curiously tiled water-tank, and the surrounding buildings were devoted to cheese-making, butter and dairy-work. . . . Outside the private dwelling are the fire-proof granaries and sheds. Night and day a sentry is stationed on the flat roof on the look out for fire and robbers, and the large double entrance-doors are always closed and barred, if the doorkeeper leaves his post; all the windows have strong iron gratings over them, after the Spanish fashion.

Because Brocklehurst prided himself on his impartiality, he also described the dwellings of the peons. These were situated 'in a long row, at some distance from the main buildings. Each family had one room, some fourteen feet square. There was a stone for a fireplace in the corner, but no chimney, no windows. The family slept on mats on the bare ground; in the daytime they lived in the open air . . .'. Far worse conditions were recorded in *Barbarous Mexico* by John Kenneth Turner, a North American journalist and socialist. Published in 1910, on the eve of the Mexican Revolution, this inflammatory book described oppression and brutality on plantations and in mines. When Díaz went into exile in 1911,

Opposite *Plan view of a nineteenth-century* hacienda *in central Mexico.*
1 *Water storage unit and pump*
2 *Water trough*
3 *Laundry area*
4 *Temascal (steam bath)*
5 *School*
6 *Houses for bonded labourers*
7 *Lookout and defensive tower*
8 *Tienda de raya (estate shop)*
9 *Machine storage unit and smithy*
10 *Warehouse*
11 *Stable with water trough for mules*
12 *Stable for horses*
13 *Cattle shed*
14 *Servants' quarters*
15 *Casa grande (main house)*
16 *Administration quarters*
17 *Main office and pay window*
18 *Gardens and orchard*
19 *Main entrance*
20 *Patio de campo (work yard)*
21 *Tinacal (pulque-making hall)*
22 *Trojes (granaries)*
23 *Church*
24 *Cemetery for the landowner's family*
25 *Corrales (area for cattle)*
26 *Threshing floor*
27 *Fields*
28 *Private railway station*

seventy per cent of all arable land was held by just one per cent of the population. *Tierra y libertad* ('land and liberty') became the rallying cry of the Revolution.

During this time of turbulence, many *hacienda* buildings were sacked or destroyed. After the Revolution, during the Agrarian Reform, the disintegration of the *haciendas* continued. The system of servitude that had bound *hacendado* and *peón* for so long was broken at last. As arable land was redistributed during the 1930s and 1940s, great rural estates were fragmented and converted into *ejidos* (land held in common by communities). Today, once imposing residences and outbuildings stand roofless and abandoned, while irrigation systems lie choked by weeds. Where the devastation has been total, only the place name remains. A few working *haciendas* survive, however, although production is generally on a smaller scale than formerly. On these estates, original buildings may or may not be respected by their owners. At San José Ozumba, for example, the rare and marvellous wall on page 180 is now at risk from an alfalfa plant. Meanwhile, on landless *ex-haciendas*, buildings have been converted for use as holiday homes, hotels, restaurants and conference centres.

Early twentieth-century postcard showing a family of Chol Indians near the lowland archaeolgical site of Palenque in the state of Chiapas. One of several Maya peoples, the Chol live in humid territories where the mean annual rainfall is 3,186 mm. Vegetation is lush. This one-room dwelling, with wattle walls and a palm roof, remains the predominant house type in many Chol settlements today.

Indigenous dwellings have been less well documented than urban or *hacienda* architecture. As colonial rule became established, Spanish interest in Indian cultures declined. During the seventeenth and eighteenth centuries, there were few descriptions or illustrations of native houses. Thomas Gage's evocation of Guatemalan habitations, published in 1648, applies equally to those of the Mexican Maya:

> Their houses are but poor thatched cottages, without any upper rooms, but commonly only one or two rooms below; they dress their meat [food] in the middle of one, and they make a compass for fire with two or three stones, without any chimney to convey the smoke away. This spreadeth itself about the room and filleth the thatch and the rafters so with soot that all the room seemeth to be a chimney. The next room, where sometimes are four or five beds according to the family, is also not free from smoke and blackness. The poorer sort have but one room, where they eat, dress their meat, and sleep. Few there are that set any locks upon their doors, for they fear no robbing nor stealing, neither have they in their houses much to lose, earthen pots, and pans, and dishes, and cups to drink their chocolate being the chief commodities in their house. There is scarce any house which hath not also in the yard a stew [*temascal*, or sweat house], wherein they bathe themselves with hot water, which is their chief physic when they feel themselves distempered.

Fortunately for the study of indigenous traditions, scenes from rural life were represented during the nineteenth century by such artists as Carlos Nebel, Johann Moritz Rugendas and Edouardo Pingret. The following account, written by Carl Sartorius *c*.1850, provides a composite view of an Indian interior in central Mexico:

> Inside the hut, upon a floor of earth just as nature formed it, burns day and night the sacred fire of the domestic hearth. Near it, stand the *metate* and

metapile, a flat and cylindrical stone for crushing the maize, and the earthen pots and dishes, a large water pitcher, a drinking cup and a dipper of gourd-shell constitute the whole wealth of the Indian's cottage, a few rude carvings, representing the saints, the decoration. Neither table nor benches cumber the room within, mats of rushes or palm leaves answer for both seat and table. They serve as beds too for their rest at night, and for their final rest in the grave.

For Carl Sartorius, Indians stood 'at the lowest point of intellectual development'. Their traditionalism was criticized by Mexicans and non-Mexicans alike. The comments of Sir Edward B. Tylor were typical of many when he wrote in 1861 of 'obstinate conservatism' in the face of 'progress' by people who 'hardly understand any reason for what they do, except that their ancestors did things so'. But the end of the nineteenth century brought a new type of observer, with different priorities. Carl Lumholtz, the Norwegian anthropologist, travelled in remote regions and spent long periods of time with the Huichol and other peoples. *Unknown Mexico*, published in 1902, included accounts of contemporary temples and dwellings, and described the customs of the seasonally nomadic Tarahumara who reside high in the Sierra Madre. 'Although it may be said that houses are their main habitations', wrote Lumholtz, 'still the Tarahumares live in caves to such an extent that they may fitly be called the American cave-dwellers of the present age.' His admiration for Mexico's indigenous peoples was clearly expressed: 'In the present rapid development of Mexico it cannot be prevented that these primitive people will soon disappear by fusion with the great nation to whom they belong . . . but I hope that I shall have rendered them a service by setting them this modest monument, and that civilised man will be the better for knowing of them.'

Nearly a century later, 56 indigenous peoples survive in Mexico. It is hard to obtain reliable census figures in harsh and isolated regions, but the Indian population is currently estimated at around 12 million, or fifteen per cent of the total. While speakers of Náhuatl (the Aztec language) exceed one million, some native languages are spoken by just a few hundred individuals. The pressures of twentieth-century modernization have affected Indian communities in different ways. Some have been absorbed into the national culture, but most continue to lead a marginal existence and retain a strong sense of identity.

Settlement patterns vary. Many peoples favour close-knit villages, but others live in family units scattered over vast distances. As in ancient times, the staple diet is composed of beans, squash, chilli peppers and maize. Although most groups today are nominal Catholics, beliefs and ceremonies frequently hark back to the traditions of their ancestors. Continuity with the past is further reflected by crafts such as weaving and basketry, and by indigenous forms of domestic

architecture. Ideally suited to environmental and climatic conditions, these vary widely from region to region.

Mexico is a land of contrasts. Tropical areas with heavy rainfall are located to the south of the Tropic of Cancer, along the Gulf Coast and the Pacific Coast. Here, houses frequently have sharply inclined roofs thatched with palm or *zacate* (grass). Leaf ends must be secured so that winds will not whip them out of position. Overhanging eaves protect walls of wattle-and-daub, poles or planks from the sun's rays and from erosion by rain. Where high roofs allow warm air to rise, the living area beneath remains cool even at the hottest period of the day. Windows are rare, but breezes enter through doorways, gaps in walls and openings at roof level. Although houses are usually rectangular or square (see page 61), circular forms occur in some regions (see ill. 6); apsidal houses are current among the Maya of Yucatán (see ill. 7).

North of the Tropic of Cancer, there is strong sunlight and low rainfall throughout most of the year. These conditions also apply in low-lying areas of Zacatecas, San Luis Potosí, Querétaro, Jalisco and Hidalgo. Because trees are scarce and vegetation limited, dwellings are chiefly made from stone, bricks or adobe (see ill. 34). Adobe-makers habitually mix straw or manure with mud for greater elasticity; the mud is then moulded in a rectangular wooden frame, and left to harden. Dry adobes are joined together with more mud, and sometimes reinforced with *rajuela* (small pebbles); walls usually rest on a foundation of stones. Rough plaster, which offers protection against insects and the elements, is made with lime (calcium oxide), water and sand; glutinous liquid from the *nopal* (prickly pear) may also be added. The Mezquital Valley in the state of Hidalgo is arid and inhospitable, but the *maguey (Agave americana)* provides Otomí inhabitants with building materials (see pages 64–5, and ill. 283). *Ocotillo*, a spiny desert shrub which flowers during the rainy season, is also used by the Otomí for house walls and fencing (see ill. 39).

Temperate zones engender the most varied architecture. On the *altiplano* (central plateau), in high valleys and low *sierras* (mountain ranges), houses frequently resemble those found in tropical or dry landscapes. Adobe is popular with Zapotec builders: in the Valley of Oaxaca, rooms open onto an interior

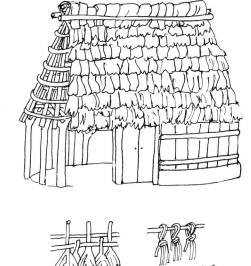

patio (see ill. 22). Where conifers and other trees abound, wooden houses are common (see ill. 27). The Purépecha of Michoacán employ heavy planks and watertight shingles or terracotta roof-tiles. Houses sit some 45–50 cm (18–20 ins) above the earth on heavy beams resting on stones (see ills. 16, 28 and 29). Such constructions are easily dismantled and rebuilt on another site.

In Indian Mexico, house-building is often a communal activity. Assistance is given by relatives, neighbours and friends. Sometimes, family obligations apply: in the Lacandón community of Najá, for example, a son-in-law is usually required after marriage to build a new house for his bride's parents. Once the ground has been levelled and the materials prepared, building operations may take just a few days. New-house ceremonies occur in a number of villages. *Modern Maya Houses: A Study of their Archaeological Significance*, written by Robert Wauchope and published in 1938, includes the following information for Tizimin, Yucatán. 'When a house is completed a hole is dug in the centre of the floor and in it are placed some holy water, a sacrificed chicken, and some silver. Prayers are then offered for the safety of the house and its occupants. Incense is burned in the hole in order that the smoke may drive away evil spirits. The cache in the floor is then sealed with marl and earth. The same thing is done when the first mainpost is dug.' The Maya ceremony described in 1934 by Robert Redfield took a rather different form. In the Yucatec village of Chan Kom, the house was regarded as an object of propitiation: sacrificial foods and drink were offered successively to different parts of the house framing. Such practices are probably very ancient.

One-room house interior in the Maya village of Chan Kom, Yucatán. Within this apsidal space, enclosed by stockade walls and protected by a thatched roof, the family sleeps, cooks, eats, rests and worships. As in pre-Hispanic times, there are few furnishings. Cooking utensils and household pottery are located near the hearth at one end of the house. Belongings such as clothes, tables and chests are stored at the other. The centre of the house is occupied by hammocks, benches, low stools and other objects. Most Maya houses have a family altar, or shrine.

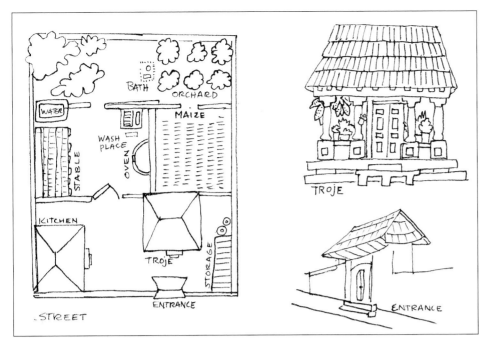

More usually, houses are blessed by the village priest. The following account was given in 1992 by an informant from the state of Tlaxcala: 'When a house is newly built, we first install the family saints. Then we go in search of the *padrino de la casa* (godfather of the house). He buys flowers and incense, and he pays the priest to bless the house. The priest sprinkles holy water in the four corners, and on family members while they kneel in prayer. The *padrino* then provides those present with biscuits and alcohol. Seven days later there is a party, as if for a wedding. The *padrino* pays the musicians. Everyone eats, drinks and celebrates far into the night.' Similar events are described in other regions. On 3 May, *Día de la Santa Cruz* (Day of the Holy Cross), villagers adorn newly finished houses with crosses and flowers.

As in pre-Conquest times, most houses have a *solar* (yard). Outdoor structures include sheds for livestock, chicken coops, covered cooking areas and sometimes a *temascal*, or indigenous steam bath (see ill. 80). 'It is low, squat . . . with a navel-like opening,' Sahagún noted in the *Historia general de las cosas de Nueva*

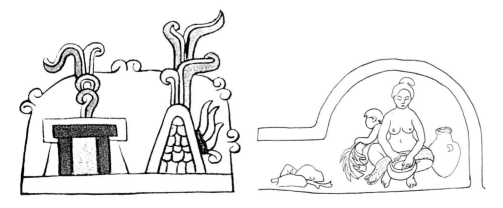

Pre-Conquest styles of corncrib. Above left Aztec bin filled with maize grains. From the Codex Magliabecchiano *(c. 1553). Above right A conquistador, by permission of the Tlaxcalans, climbs a ladder to collect maize cobs for the Spanish army. From the* Lienzo de Tlaxcala *(1550–64).*

España (*c.* 1540–77): 'There is bathing, there are washing, cleansing and the holding of vigils.' Today, curative powers are still attributed to the *temascal.* Steam baths are thought by the Nahua, the Otomí and many other peoples to alleviate rheumatism and to hasten recovery after illness and childbirth. According to one user in Tlaxcala, 'the heat is intense. In our house, we bathe this way each Saturday. Modern showers only clean you on the outside, but the *temescal* will clean you inside as well.' Granaries also have a long history in Mexico. As with houses, forms and building techniques are variable (see pages 92–5). If properly maintained, vasiform corncribs in the state of Morelos last sixty years or more; sometimes new granaries are blessed by the priest and adorned with a cross.

In recent years 'sophisticated' architects have begun increasingly to incorporate traditional elements and natural materials into their designs. Handsome holiday retreats for wealthy city-dwellers now feature adobe walls and thatched roofs. Rural builders, on the other hand, are abandoning traditional styles in favour of concrete and corrugated iron. At a time when traditional Mexican architecture is under threat, this book seeks to document the achievements of Mexico's builders, past and present.

Three generations outside a family house in the Mazahua village of San Simón de la Laguna, Mexico State. An overhanging roof of terracotta tiles protects the plank walls from rain. Seen here is the outer wall of the kitchen; additional rooms extend to the sides. The house is surrounded by open land where domestic and agricultural tasks are performed. The extended family will build new dwellings around the parental home.

1

USING COLOUR

TRAVEL BROCHURES invariably present Mexico as a land of colour. Luscious fruits, flowering trees, vivid sunsets, painted walls and rainbow blankets are a major attraction for modern tourists. Such vibrancy does not suit all tastes, however. In 1911, Mary Barton (English visitor and author of *Impressions of Mexico with Brush and Pen*) confided to her readers that Mexicans 'are fond of colour, but have not the fine sense of it. . . . The tints with which they paint their houses are crude until toned down by the summer rains . . .'. She was troubled by skirts dyed 'a horrible bluish-pink of a most unpleasant brilliancy'. Even the bougainvillaea was deemed to cause 'more distress than pleasure to the artist': 'it seems to harmonise with nothing and is so strong in tone that it positively jumps at one from supporting walls, with its almost leafless abundance of crude colour'.

Since Mary Barton's visit, the Mexican enjoyment of colour has intensified still further. Brilliantly coloured plastics and clothing of rayon and acrylic are displayed beside more traditional wares in Mexican markets; improved communications have taken factory-produced paints to the remotest regions of the country. Inner and outer house-walls, ceilings and even graves resonate with colour in many villages, while saints in tiny churches gaze out from niches of *rosa mexicano* (shocking pink). In poor homes with few furnishings, colour is often the only luxury.

The juxtaposition of strong colours is now a feature of much sophisticated urban architecture. Since 1940, the broad, intersecting wall planes of Luis Barragán (1902–88) and, more recently, Ricardo Legorreta, have been increasingly defined by colour. Provincial towns, with their brightly painted walls, were a never-ending source of inspiration. Interviewed in 1976 by Elena Poniatowska, Barragán stated 'my chief influence is popular architecture', and talked about the origins of his sensual colour range: 'My roots are in Mexico; I had the good fortune to live in the countryside, in small villages. . . . When I use a strong colour like red or purple, it is because my mind has suddenly been illuminated by the memory of some Mexican festival, some stall in some market, the brilliance of a fruit, a watermelon or a wooden horse. . . . In Mexico people invent colours: in Pátzcuaro there are pinks and reds; Huejotzingo also has marvellous colours – indigo blue, plaster white – this is timeless architecture which will never outlive its period because it belongs to no period . . .'.

The use of colour in architecture goes back to pre-Hispanic times. As discussed in the Introduction, cities such as Teotihuacán, Tula, Chichén Itzá and Tenoch-

Opposite **Libres, Puebla** *House-owners in rural Mexico often personalize their homes by painting façades and inside walls with bright colours. Maurilio López Rosales has developed his own unique style of decoration. Outside walls are painted anew each year (see p. 47, below); interior walls are adorned with figurative and abstract designs.*

39

titlan were elaborately painted with vegetable and mineral colorants. Pyramids, temples, civic buildings and palaces carried polychromatic sculptural reliefs, while inside walls displayed frescoed images of gods, priests and religious symbols. After the Conquest, church murals – some executed by Indian artists working under the direction of friars – reflected Christian themes for the instruction and enlightenment of Spain's new subjects. With the full flowering of Mexican Baroque in the eighteenth century, glazed tiles brought colour to ecclesiastical and domestic buildings in the state of Puebla, covering façades, cupolas, fountains and kitchen walls.

Nineteenth-century Mexico attracted a host of foreign visitors. Thomas Unett Brocklehurst, who visited the capital in 1881, described the 'gay appearance' of the houses: 'such as are not white or light yellow or green are tinted with various shades of red, and many of the churches may be pronounced pink; three or four hundred yards of a street in pink has a pretty effect, especially if continued in pale green; a house in grey stone adjoining another faced with blue encaustic tiles is, to say the least, pleasing to the eye. . . . As you get into the outskirts of the city the houses are meaner, but many of them are festooned with flowers and wreaths, so the appearance of beauty is maintained, even if on close inspection it is found delusive.'

In the countryside, *haciendas* could also be colourful. Emma Lindsay Squier and her husband were guests at San Antonio Ometusco in the state of Mexico. From the railway station, the complex appeared to them like a 'salmon-pink birthday cake in the shape of a walled fortress'. Mural panels in *haciendas* and wealthy town-houses copied European models: star-crossed lovers, British hunting scenes and landscapes with peacocks were recurrent themes.

The mural movement, born of the 1910 Revolution, reflected the search for a Mexican identity and espoused the cause of public art. From 1920 onwards, artists such as Diego Rivera travelled the country studying murals in pre-Hispanic sites and colonial monasteries, as well as painted decorations in shops, restaurants and *pulquerías*. Today, painted walls are still a popular form of self-expression. Maurilio López Rosales, whose home appears on page 47, received no formal art training: 'I left school at twelve; now I mend radios and television sets. I don't know why I feel the need to paint. I've never travelled or looked at books. Each year I decorate the front of my house for the Feast of the Assumption. Inside, I pattern the cement floors to look like carpets, and cover the walls with my designs. Where my ideas come from, who can say. Even as a child, I liked bright colours. When I started this, some of the neighbours said that I was mad. Even my family disapproved: they complained that I was wasting money on paints. Now they accept what I do. I don't want to offend people. I just want my work to be unique.'

Opposite *Santa María Canchzdé, Mexico State* Baroque church with brightly painted ornamentation in stucco. In many regions of Mexico the Baroque style of architecture and decoration lasted until the late eighteenth century and beyond. Inspired by city architecture, the builders of rural churches often brought a joyous exuberance to their work.

Opposite **Tlacotalpan, Veracruz**
*Colonial-style window with white-painted
surround. The* reja *(grille) forms a tiny,
enclosed porch. Moorish in origin, it
safeguards the security of the house, while
providing light and ventilation; it also
allows the inhabitants to remain in touch
with the street, as people can chat through
the bars.*

Right **La Unión, Puebla** *Bright colours,
in striking combinations, enliven the streets
of rural Mexico. Here, a roughly plastered
wall and wooden door have been coated
with paint.*

Below **Tlacotalpan, Veracruz** *One-storey
house embellished with stucco; the pilasters
and fan-shaped decorations above the door
and windows are emphasized with white
paint. The wall and even the waterspouts
are painted* rosa mexicano *(Mexican pink).*

Left **San José Miahuatlán, Puebla** Detail of a village quiosco (bandstand). The underside of the roof has been painted with local views, pre-Hispanic figures and a maize ear. Seen in the centre is a Nahua couple wearing indigenous dress.

Below **Rafael L. Grajales, Puebla** Small shops and restaurants often display hand-painted advertisements to publicize the goods and services on offer. Here, a painted tiger promotes the sale of Bicicletas el Tigre. It was executed by the shop-owner's son, José-Luis Júarez Santos (seen below). He works inside selling bicycles and mending television sets.

Opposite **San Bartolomé, Michoacán** Mazahua woman in regional clothing outside the vestry that adjoins the village church. Walls are thickly coated with plaster. The cement floor and wooden ceiling project to form a veranda. Column capitals are decoratively carved.

Opposite **Alvarado, Veracruz** The inhabitants of Alvarado, like those of most Mexican towns and villages, take great pride in their zócalo (main square). Glazed tiles adorn walls, walkways and the benches that curve behind the twentieth-century quiosco. Families and courting couples come to the zócalo in the evenings and at weekends to stroll, sit, listen to music and eat ice-cream.

Right **Ciudad del Carmen, Campeche** Fashionable small-town houses built and eclectically decorated during the Porfirian era (1876–1911). Elegant pilasters and ornamental work in stucco testified to the relative wealth of their owners.

Below **Libres, Puebla** Outer wall enclosing a house and patio. Each year it is painted with different designs and increasing zest by Maurilio López Rosales. Neighbours and relatives react in different ways to this ever-changing artwork. Some see it as an asset to the barrio; others view it as an eyesore, and grumble about the money that Maurilio spends on materials.

Left **Zacazacata, Puebla** *Colonial church doorway. Masonry walls are thickly coated with plaster. The opening is framed by a semicircular arch.*

Below **San Antonio Ometusco, Mexico State** *Until the Revolution of 1910* haciendas *operated as autonomous, essentially feudal estates. San Antonio Ometusco depended on the production of* pulque – *an intoxicating drink made by fermenting the sweet sap of* Agave atrovirens *and some other large species of* maguey. *Built in imposing fashion, this* tienda de raya, *or estate shop, was completed in 1890. Here, peons were entrapped in a web of debts for the purchase of basic necessities.*

Opposite **Cuitzeo, Michoacán** *Public building from the colonial period. Glimpsed through a succession of archways, the patio suggests a Moorish courtyard.*

Left **San Antonio Ometusco, Mexico State** The tinacal, or great pulque-*making hall, of the* hacienda *also served as office and bank. Shown here is the wooden pay-booth where labourers received their wages. Murals, executed in 1885 by Andrés Padilla y Mala, evoke the history of* pulque; *above the booth, rays of light emanate from the all-seeing eye of God.*

Below **Micuatla, Puebla** *During the Porfirian era, many* haciendas *were substantially re-modelled and enlarged. European styles of decoration were much in vogue, and interiors were designed for maximum splendour. This once opulent reception room boasted tiled floors, a crystal chandelier and costly imported furniture. Walls were painted with European scenes.*

Opposite **San Antonio Ometusco, Mexico State** *Detail of the doorway of the great house. Glazed tiles were imported from England; statues were carved in Paris.*

Opposite *Mérida, Yucatán* Family
mansion from the Porfirian era, opulently
decorated inside and out. The architect has
combined rococo, neo-classical and neo-
Baroque styles. During the nineteenth
century sisal plantations generated huge
fortunes for their owners. Many built town
houses in the city of Mérida, giving it a
European aura that it retains today.

Right *Hoctún, Yucatán* In Mexico death
is seen as a part of life. 'Only those who
are never born will never become skulls',
runs one popular saying. In this Maya
cemetery tombs, shaped like miniatur
houses and churches, are lovingly painted
by villagers.

Below *Pueblo Nuevo, Mexico State*
Mazahua cemetery during the Festival of
the Dead; graves have been tidied and
colourfully painted to welcome returning
souls. On the morning of 2 November (All
Souls' Day) villagers visit the tombs of dead
relatives with offerings of marigolds,
candles and incense.

Left **Tlacotalpan, Veracruz** Wrought-iron door-knocker in the form of a hand; a serpent serves as a bracelet. Although fine ironwork is still executed in several regions, older examples are avidly sought by collectors.

Below **La Trinidad, Puebla** Eighteenth-century rural church in Baroque style. In the state of Puebla, walls were often faced with glazed tiles. The use and manufacture of azulejos (glazed polychrome tiles) were introduced into Mexico by Spanish settlers. Today, Puebla City remains an important centre for the production of tiles.

Opposite **San Juan Teposcolula, Oaxaca** Ayuntamiento, or seat of local government. The ornate façade was completed in 1929. It displays the national emblem of Mexico: an eagle perched on a prickly pear cactus.

2

RURAL HOUSES

ARCHITECTURAL HISTORIANS have tended, in the past, to concentrate on 'formal' architecture. *Architecture without Architects* was the title chosen in 1964 by Bernard Rudofsky for a pioneering exhibition at the Museum of Modern Art in New York. He outlined his aims in the accompanying book: '*Architecture without Architects* attempts to break down our narrow concepts of the art of building by introducing the unfamiliar world of nonpedigreed architecture. It is so little known that we don't even have a name for it. For want of a generic label, we shall call it vernacular, anonymous, spontaneous, indigenous, rural, as the case may be.... The beauty of this architecture has long been dismissed as accidental, but today we should be able to recognize it as the result of rare good sense in the handling of practical problems. The shapes of the houses, sometimes transmitted through a hundred generations, seem eternally valid, like those of their tools.'

As the following photographs show, Mexico's widely varying geography has fostered an extensive range of architectural solutions. Fertile valleys, tropical lowland forests, arid deserts, high mountain peaks and deep canyons make up a land of extreme contrasts. Despite the lure of towns and cities, nearly half of Mexico's estimated ninety million inhabitants still live in rural areas and work the land. Recently built roads now link different parts of the country, but the ruggedness of the terrain has proved a major obstacle to modernization in many places.

Indian peoples in remote settlements often lead a surprisingly marginal existence. Continuity with the past is reflected in numerous ways. Natural surroundings provide the Nahua, the Amusgo, the Tzotzil, the Tzeltal and other indigenous groups with raw materials for ancient crafts such as pot-making, textile-weaving and basketry; they also supply elements for house-building. Perfectly adapted to their environment, traditional dwellings may incorporate palm or grass for thatching, wattle, agave spikes, wood, stone and adobe (sun-dried mud blocks). Terracotta roof-tiles and kiln-fired bricks, in wide use in Spain, are also employed by Indian house-builders.

House forms, determined by topography and climate, are square, rectangular, apsidal or round. Roofs may be flat, *de un agua* (slanting), *de dos aguas* (with two slopes), *de cuatro aguas* (with four slopes), apsidal or conical; they incline steeply in rainy areas, and overhang to protect walls from erosion. Dwellings consist of one or more rooms. Floors are mainly of pressed earth, and interiors

Opposite *Cosoleacaque, Veracruz* *Palm-thatched houses in this Nahua village are constructed in approximately one week. Wattle walls are daubed with clay; air circulates through open doors and the occasional square window. The extended family build around the parental home to form clusters of earth-coloured dwellings, which merge into the luxuriant landscape.*

are sparsely furnished. Because windows are small and admit little light, most activities take place outside in the *solar* (yard). Additional structures include granaries or maize cribs, pens for animals, and sometimes a *temascal* (steam bath). In many regions, houses are tightly grouped and aligned to form streets; in others, they are irregularly dispersed throughout the landscape.

Totonac farmers who live among the tree-covered hills of lowland Veracruz build their houses in small clearings, well hidden from view and remote from one another. Pedro Martínez García lives with his extended family near the archaeological site of El Tajín. 'My parents and my grandparents made their home in this place. Our land gives us maize, squash, beans, chiles, *cacao*, sugarcane, limes and vanilla. We keep chickens and pigs. I built this house myself, with the help of my brothers and my sons, and we feel happy here. We have a palm roof and plank walls. When the roof wears out, I will replace it. There are draughts during the cold months, but the house stays cool when the weather is hot. When my eldest son marries, I will help him build a house nearby.' Made from local materials, such houses are inexpensive. They are also relatively easy to dismantle and reassemble if the inhabitants decide to move to another part of the clearing.

Thatched roofs last approximately ten years; walls of stakes, planks or wattle-and-daub last considerably longer if protected from rainfall. Adobe houses with tiled roofs often shelter numerous generations, however. Widely used in Mexico by Indians and *mestizos*, sun-dried bricks keep interiors cool in summer and warm in cold weather. In many villages in the Valley of Oaxaca and elsewhere, inhabitants live behind high adobe walls: rooms open on to a central yard replete with flowers and foliage. Handsome wrought-iron window-grilles, which safeguard security while allowing light and air to enter, distinguish plastered and painted façades of brick or adobe in non-Indian communities such as Tlacotalpan and Xico in Veracruz, or Mina in Nuevo León.

Strong emotional and spiritual ties bind families to their houses and their land. Most births and deaths take place in the intimacy of the home, in view of the family altar with its holy images and representations of Catholic saints. As we saw in the Introduction, building practices, beliefs and associated rituals – some, without doubt, extremely ancient – persist in several regions. Many ceremonies are thought to protect the house, and to ensure the health and happiness of the inhabitants.

Cultural values and traditional styles of architecture are now being widely challenged, however. As communications improve, villagers from isolated communities become ever more aware of city fashions. Travel and television foster new aspirations, and indigenous customs are increasingly perceived as 'backward' by those who practise them. For many 'progressive' Indians, home-woven garments and thatched houses are a source of shame and embarrassment, while synthetic fabrics, plastics and the breezeblock are seen as symbols of modernity.

Now in her sixties, María Cruz Angela Ramírez speaks Spanish and Otomí, and lives in González y González in the state of Hidalgo: 'In this region, which is hot and dry, we used to build our houses from *maguey* [agave] spikes. They would last twenty years or more, and the interiors were always cool. But few people today want to live in such houses. Mine is the only one left in this place. Over there, as you can see, my son has built a modern house. He went to work in the USA, and when he came back he made his house with walls of breezeblock and a roof of *lámina* [corrugated sheet-metal]. I live there with him, but when the sun beats down on the roof we feel hot and uncomfortable. That is why I keep my old house. I use it to cook in, and it is always cool. Yet no one likes these houses any more. Everyone here remembers how to build them, but I do not think that any more will be built.' Houses of the type described here are shown on pages 64, 65 and 192.

Also represented in this book are several other architectural traditions which seem doomed to extinction. This same trend towards standardization has overtaken most countries in the world, yet it will be a sad reflection on 'progress' if ancient house-building techniques are lost to future generations. Mexico urgently needs to establish a museum of vernacular architecture, while she is fortunate enough to have rural builders who know how to live in harmony with the natural environment, and who still possess the wisdom and practical skills of their ancestors.

1△ 2▽ 3▽

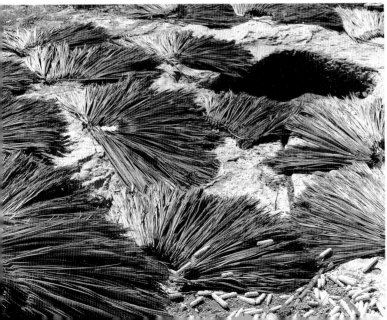

House-builders in many regions still make use of natural materials; these include local species of palm or grass for thatching. Roof forms vary widely.   **1 Tekom, Yucatán** Apsidal roofs are common among the Maya of Yucatán. The thatch must be watertight at the crest so that rainwater will roll down the roof slopes.   **2 El Calvario, Puebla** Fan-shaped fronds from the palma real drying in the sun before use.

3 Chinameca, Morelos Detail of a conical roof-frame in a Nahua village.

4 Cosoleacaque, Veracruz Nahua houses here are small and rectangular, with gently rounded corners. The overhanging palm roof protects the walls from erosion (see also p. 56).   **5 San Felipe Usila, Oaxaca** Rectangular Chinantec house. Windowless plank walls stand on a base of river stones. The very high hip roof, thatched with grass and steeply inclined, protrudes some 1.2 m (4 ft) over the walls. The ridge pole has a covering of thatch to protect the jointure of the two main roof slopes. Openings at each end provide ventilation in the hot climate.

4 △

5 △

6 San Pedro Amusgos, Oaxaca Round, windowless houses are common in Amusgo villages, where days are hot and nights are cool. Thatched with grass, the conical roof is constructed on the ground, then raised to rest on eight or ten mainposts arranged in a circle. An inverted pot is usually positioned on the top to prevent rain from entering at the apex. Walls of bajareque (wattle-and-daub) are approximately 3 m (10ft) high. Some families, as here, cook in one structure and sleep in a second.

7 Yaxcabá, Yucatán Maya house-builders in Yucatán often construct a small platform substructure with limestone rocks and mortar; this prevents subsidence after heavy rain and protects the vertical wooden poles, lashed together to form the walls, from rotting at their base. The apsidal roof is thatched with palm to form overhanging eaves (see also p. 76).

6△ 7▽

8 **Tenejapa, Chiapas** *Square Tzeltal house. Thatched with zacate (grass), the pyramidal roof rises to nearly three times the height of the walls; firewood is stored along the outer walls.* 9 **El Carmen Tequexquitla, Tlaxcala** *This style of house-building, uniquely employed by the Nahua of El Carmen Tequexquitla, is now increasingly rare. Vertical and horizontal poles are lashed together to form the framework. The ridge pole extends the whole length of the house. Bundles of sun-dried rye stalks, anchored to horizontal rods, are positioned in overlapping layers.*

8△ 9▽

10△ 11▽

The environment of the Mezquital Valley is arid and inhospitable, yet the Otomí who live there have relied for centuries on the maguey, or Mexican agave, for house-building materials, natural fencing, food and sweet sap, soap pulp and coarse fibres. **10 Santiago de Anaya, Hidalgo Detail of a** maguey house. Equipped at either end with an air vent (shown here), the roof descends to the ground to form the side walls. Agave spikes are folded over horizontal rods in closely overlapping layers. Houses made by this method last an average of twenty years. **11 Hidalgo** Maguey (Agave americana): *freshly severed spikes are brittle because of the moisture they contain; after they have been dried in the sun, they become flexible.*

12△ 13▽

12 **Hermosillo, Hidalgo** Maguey *roof seen from the interior, which remains fresh and cool even when the sun is at its zenith. The beams and poles of the house are made from the* quiotes *(flower stalks) of the maguey. Elements are tied together with* ixtle *(maguey fibres).* 13 **González Ortega, Hidalgo** *Rectangular house. The walls of dry rubble masonry and adobe bricks were built more than thirty years ago, but the gabled roof of agave spikes has recently been renovated.*

14△　15▽　　　　　　　　　　　　　　16▽

14 Santa María Jaltianguis, Oaxaca
Because rainwater runs off tiled roofs with ease, they tend to incline less steeply than thatched ones. Terracotta tiles are made in various shapes, but the teja árabe acanalada (Spanish tile) is the type most commonly used, as here. **15 Magueyitos, Veracruz** Wooden house under construction. Sheets of lámina (corrugated metal) are being nailed to the framing of the four-sided roof. The walls, formed by roughly hewn, horizontal planks, rest on a base of horizontal logs over stones.

16 Ocumicho, Michoacán The Purépecha of Michoacán are famed for their handsomely finished houses of wooden planks and shingles (see also ills. 28 and 29). Such constructions are easily dismantled and rebuilt on another site.

Roofing details. **17 Olinalá, Guerrero** Decoratively painted pillar supporting a flat, layered roof of terrado: earth, with sand and lime, is laid beneath the tiles on a 'bed' of otate (Mexican bamboo).

18 Escamilla, Querétaro Thatched roof seen from beneath; domestic objects often hang from the wooden framing. **19 El Carmen, Zacatecas** In desert areas of Zacatecas, the pitahaya cactus is used as a base for the terrado roof. Stalks are scraped, left to dry out, and cut into even lengths; they are then laid herringbone-fashion in neat rows. **20 El Carmen Tequexquitla, Tlaxcala** Sun-dried rye stalks are positioned in layers. **21 Santa Cecilia Jalieza, Oaxaca** Bricks, painted with sun motifs and maize plants, jut out in a row, forming a transition between the wall and the roof.

17 △

18 △

19 △

20 △

21 △

22△   23△   24▽

Building with adobe (sun-dried mud bricks) is especially common in arid and semi-arid regions, where insulation is required against daytime heat and night-time cold.

22 Santo Domingo Jalieza, Oaxaca Zapotec village dwelling. The houses have no windows onto the street. Walls of adobe bricks rest on a foundation of stones; roofs have a single incline. **23 Magdalena Apasco, Oaxaca** Flat-roofed house, to which a lean-to kitchen has been added. The ends of the projecting wooden roof-beams are carved. **24 San Francisco Xochitepec, Puebla** One-room house with a tiled roof. Similar constructions are widely found in central and northern Mexico. **25 Huaquechula, Puebla** The stone base and door- and window-frames lend solidity to the adobe structures of Huaquechula, founded soon after the Spanish Conquest. **26 San Mateo, Mexico State** The height of these gabled roofs, protected by flat oriada (fish-scale) tiles, is equal to that of the massive adobe walls beneath.

25 △

26 △

Although deforestation is increasing in some areas of Mexico, others remain rich in trees. Rural house-builders in states such as Michoacán still rely on planks, logs, stakes and shingles. **27 Metepec, Hidalgo** Dwelling made from heavy logs, notched to interlock at the corners and secured by pressure alone. **28 Ocumicho, Michoacán** This type of dwelling, known as a *troje*, is made from heavy planks. Floor and ceiling project to form a veranda (see also ill. 64). **29 San Felipe de los Herreros, Michoacán** Roofs in this Purépecha village are covered with watertight wooden shingles.

Houses and boundary walls are often made of dry-laid stones. Large, irregular rocks are held in place by stone chippings inserted into the crevices between them. Elsewhere, quarried stone may be hewn by masons. **30 San Marcos, Guanajuato** A thatched roof covers this simple dwelling. During the day the sun heats the stones, which slowly release warmth throughout the night. **31 San Mateo, Guanajuato** Dry-laid stone walls enclose patio, rooms and stables. **32 Real del Catorce, San Luis Potosí** In this once thriving mining town, massive houses, stairways and pavements were assembled from stones and mortar; wooden beams serve as lintels for doors and windows. Ramps and stairs follow the irregular topography.

27 △

28 △

29 △

30△

31△ 32▽

33 Copales, Sinaloa Detail of a Mayo house. Insulation is aided by air pockets, trapped between the different materials that make up the various roof layers. The living area below remains fresh and cool, even during the hottest period of the day.

34 Acámbaro Viejo, Coahuila Typical adobe house found in the northern states, where the climate is extreme. A huge fireplace is used for heating and cooking. Old-style wagons are still used by the inhabitants when travelling from one ranch to another.

33 △   34 ▽

Constructions of rammed earth, formed in sections. Vertical plank frames, supported by wooden poles, are positioned in situ and packed with earth. When the earth is dry, the mould is removed, leaving a strong section of wall. **35 Magueyitos, Veracruz** *Boundary wall, with clearly visible joins. Sections are staggered for greater stability.* **36 La Unión, Puebla** *The walls of this simple house are made of rammed earth. The roof overhangs the walls to protect them from the rain.*

35△   36▽

37△ 38▽   39▽

37 La Loma de Echarropa, Sonora *The overhanging thatched roof, supported by stout log posts, creates an area of shade in front of this one-room house. Many household tasks are performed outdoors.*
38 Etchojoa, Sonora *Detail of a wattle construction where Mayo women prepare food.*

Boundary walls and fences are created in countless ways in rural Mexico.
39 Orizabita, Hidalgo *Ocotillo is a spiny desert shrub; used for fencing and house-building by many Otomí, it flowers during the rainy season.* **40 Atla, Puebla** *Stick fences follow the line of the hillside in this Nahua village.* **41 Mina, Nuevo León** *Large stones, shaped by a mason, form the lower part of this wall; chinks are filled in with smaller stones. Adobe bricks make up the top part.* **42 Etla, Oaxaca** *In the Valley of Oaxaca, a Zapotec villager interweaves lengths of* otate, *commonly known as Mexican bamboo.*
43 Portezuelo, Hidalgo *A line of* órganos *forms a natural cactus fence.*

40 △

41 △

42 △

43 △

House-walls are often coated with rough plaster. **44 San Pedro Amusgos, Oaxaca** Rectangular dwelling with a tiled roof weighted down by stones. Houses of this type, which are mestizo in inspiration, are supplanting the round house of wattle-and-daub that once predominated among the Amusgo (see ill. 6). **45 Pomuch, Campeche** Apsidal Maya house of rubble masonry, built on a platform substructure and enclosed by a low entrance wall. **46 Sisal, Yucatán** Simple, flat-roofed house with a front garden. As in colonial times, door and window apertures are emphasized by a band of colour. **47 Pinos, Zacatecas** Stained by rainwater, the plaster coating has flaked away to reveal the fired bricks beneath. **48 Chila, Puebla** Here, benches have a dual function. As part of the structure, they stabilize the outer wall, which has been partially restored with cement; they also allow people to sit and watch the street. The flat roof is equipped with waterspouts.

44 △

45 △

46△   47△   48▽

49△ 50▽

Decorative elements range from the traditional to the highly personal.

49 Mina, Nuevo León A reja (grille) of wrought iron with lead arrow-points protects the window. In the seventeenth and eighteenth centuries, window and door jambs were often carried up to the roof as decorative elements and emphasized with paint, as they are here. The guardapolvos, or skirting of paint along the base of the wall, is another time-honoured feature.

50 Nautla, Veracruz Colour is provided by the guardapolvos and matching doors. A roof with flared eaves extends out on pillars to form a covered walkway, or portico.

51 Valladolid, Yucatán High-relief stripes
pattern the façade in a bold, dramatic
fashion.   **52 Mina, Nuevo León** The
inhabitants of Mina delight in bright,
contrasting colours and striking patterns.
This small, one-room house has been
embellished with geometric designs of
bright blue on a white ground.

51△   52▽

79

53△ 54▽   55▽

In desert areas windows are often non-existent or extremely small. The apertures shown here aid ventilation but admit only a small amount of light. Household tasks such as sewing are usually performed outside. **53 Terrenate, Tlaxcala** Wall covered with rough plaster. As in colonial times, the window is outlined with a wide band of paint which is usually in contrast to the colour of the wall. Wooden planks serve as a shutter. **54 El Sauz, Zacatecas** A lightbulb burns in the interior of this stone-and-mortar house. The window has a wooden lintel. **55 La Higuerita, Nayarit** The bars of otate, or Mexican bamboo, are part of the structure of the house. An opening is left where the window is desired.

Doors from several regions. **56 Jerez, Zacatecas** Interior patio of a Porfirian house. A decorative screen across the window safeguards the privacy of the inhabitants, while allowing air to circulate. Window and door embellishments are of carved wood. **57 Tlacotalpan, Veracruz** Houses along the Gulf Coast and the Caribbean Sea often have double doors – the louvred half-door allows a breeze into the room; the inner door is closed at night and during storms. **58 Santa María del Tule, Oaxaca** Massive doors decorated in eighteenth-century fashion with studded iron nails. Between the roof-tiles and the single wooden lintel is a row of ventilation holes. **59 Jerez, Zacatecas** Door-frame of smooth, dressed stone. **60 Mina, Nuevo León** A channel in the wall, in this case between the two doors, conducts the rainwater from the flat roof down to the street.

56 △

57 △

58 △

59 △

60 △

In rural house interiors floors are often of pressed earth. Where there is still no electricity, candles or kerosene lamps provide light at night. **61 Molango, Hidalgo** Religious devotion lies at the heart of rural life. Throughout the year the family altar takes pride of place in Catholic homes. Here, pictures of saints and holy images are displayed on the wall, surrounded by homemade paper flowers and decorations. **62 El Cedro, Veracruz** Totonac room hung with paper garlands before a wedding. The groom will carry the bride over the threshold.

61△ 62▽

Purépecha houses in the state of Michoacán usually have a porch where inhabitants can work or rest. **63 San Lucas, Michoacán** Inhabitants of the Yucatán peninsula often sleep in hammocks during the night. In most other regions, however, hammocks are used for daytime rest; they hang in the shade of the porch, as here, or inside the house. **64 San Felipe de los Herreros, Michoacán** Troje, or wooden dwelling, with hanging plants, carved columns and plank flooring. A homemade ladder leads up into the tapanco (loft), where maize is stored (see also ill. 28).

63△   64▽

65 △

67 △

84

66 △

Furnishings are often minimal and locally made. **65 Huaquechula, Puebla** A child's cradle of otate *hangs from the rafters; gauze-patterned factory material serves as mosquito netting.* **66 Macuilxochitl, Oaxaca** *Valued objects and infrequently used clothing are stored in this wooden chest. The adobe brick walls are untreated. Although many rural families still sleep on petates (palm mats), others prefer plank beds of the kind shown here.* **67 El Cedro, Veracruz** *Table for the preparation and eating of meals.* **68 Teotitlán del Valle, Oaxaca** *Wooden chair and bench on a tiled floor. Walls have been given a coating of plaster by the Zapotec inhabitants.* **69 El Cedro, Veracruz** *This form of chair, termed a* butaca, *is often seen in Totonac homes. In other regions it is common to find leather stretched over the wooden frame.* **70 Zacán, Michoacán** *Porch of a Purépecha* troje, *or wooden house, with a highly prized sewing machine. Daylight enables the owner to do close work.*

68△

69△ 70▽

71△   72▽

Food preparation in Mexico is labour-intensive. In remote communities water often needs to be fetched from a spring or public tap, while cooking is done with firewood on an open hearth. The basic shape of many domestic utensils has changed little in centuries. Cooking and sleeping areas are sometimes included in a single room, although larger dwellings may incorporate a separate kitchen. Sometimes an outside cooking shelter is preferred. **71 El Cedro, Veracruz** Lowland Totonac who live near Papantla favour a raised, mud-plastered hearth; this is usually built in a corner of the main house. **72 Santa Fe de la Laguna, Michoacán** Purépecha circular hearth of bricks and mortar, with a pottery comal (griddle); the palm fan is used to coax the flames.

73△ 74▽

73 **Rancho La Unión, Veracruz** *Ranch-style kitchen: cooking implements hang from walls and rafters.* 74 **Yalalag, Oaxaca** *A Zapotec woman kneels to make tortillas* in *an outside shelter of poles and thatch. As in pre-Hispanic times, maize dough is prepared on a* metate *(grinding stone); the pottery* comal *rests on a hearth of three stones.*

75△   76▽

77▽

Most rural houses have a *solar*, or yard. Domestic tasks and celebrations take place here, together with regional activities such as weaving and wood-carving. Often, agricultural produce, tools and livestock are kept on this land. **75 San Tadeo Huiloapan, Tlaxcala** Bread-oven of bricks on a base of dry rubble masonry. Wheat was introduced into Mexico during the colonial period. Although maize tortillas are eaten every day in the countryside, wheat bread has become an important food during religious festivals. **76 San Mateo del Mar, Oaxaca** Huave women washing dishes in front of their one-room house; palm fronds are weighted along the roof crest with wooden branches. **77 Metepec, Mexico State** Potter's interior patio. Maize kernels are being removed from the cob; a broken pottery bull stands in the background. **78 Tequixtepec, Oaxaca** Weddings, fifteenth birthdays and other family events are celebrated in the patio. **79 Ihuatzio, Michoacán** Wedding guests eat in the shade created by an overhanging roof. Music and dancing will follow.

78 △

79 △

80 **Vicancio, Tlaxcala** The temascal, or steam bath, has been used since pre-Hispanic times. Built from stones or adobe, its walls and roof are rendered airtight. Special stones divide the dome-shaped bathing chamber from the projecting fireplace. When the wood fire has heated the stones, they are drenched with cold water. The resulting vapour causes bathers to sweat profusely. 81 and 82 **Santo Tomás Jalieza, Oaxaca** Zapotec bathing shelter made with reeds and zacate (grasses). Water, stored in large pots, is scooped out with a dipper.

Life in many communities hinges on the cultivation of maize and other crops. Often, these are grown at some distance from the main dwelling, but fruit trees and herb plots may be found in the solar (yard). During the day, pigs and chickens roam freely. 83 **Ciénega Larga, Puebla** Agricultural storehouse of logs and shingles. 84 **Chililico, Hidalgo** One-room Nahua house with mud-covered stake walls. Protected from the elements by the overhanging thatched roof, agricultural produce is drying on a stake platform, and firewood is stacked ready for use. 85 **Pechil, Yucatán** Maya chicken coop, built like a miniature house from sticks and thatch.

80△

81△

82△

83△   84△ 85▽

Although maize is sometimes stored within the main house, outside cribs are preferred by many farmers. Forms vary from region to region. Grain must be protected from rats, insects and the elements. Ventilation stops mould attacking the maize ears while they are stored. **86 Santa María Totoltepec, Mexico State** Cincolote *with a thatched roof. In the state of Mexico unhusked maize ears are often kept in a rectangular crib. Cane walls, supported by vertical wooden poles, permit free circulation of air. The floor is raised above the earth. Maize is removed from the top of the crib with the aid of a ladder.*
87 **Temoaya, Mexico State** *The construction of a* cincolote. *This type of corncrib is disassembled once the maize has been used up, and rebuilt during the next harvest. Size varies in accordance with the amount of grain to be stored.*

86△   87▽

88 El Rosario, Tlaxcala Log granary, resting on vertical supports. The roof is of shingles. **89 Coachimilco, Guerrero** Maize ears drying on a raised platform of wooden stakes.

88△ 89▽

Structures for storing maize. **90 San Gabriel, Morelos** *Nahua cuezcomate, or vasiform granary, for shelled maize. Bundles of zacate (grass) are secured in layers to form the roof; an inverted tin can at the summit keeps out heavy rain. The walls, built up in stages from mud and straw, rest on a stone foundation. The* cuezcomate *is filled through an opening under the roof; when maize grains are needed, they run out through the* ombligo, *or navel. At other times this small channel near the base is blocked with a dry maize cob. Structures can last for several decades if properly maintained.* **91 Tepetlapa, Hidalgo** *Wooden storehouse with a hip roof of shingles.* **92 Tlaxmalac, Guerrero** *Palm-thatched granary of* bajareque (wattle-and-daub). **93 Miacatlán, Morelos** *Circular maizecrib of interwoven canes on a raised platform.* **94 El Carmen Tequexquitla, Tlaxcala** *Nahua storehouse of vertical wooden stakes; this structure has a layered roof of rye stalks (see also ills. 9 and 20).*

90△

92△ 93▽   94▽

3

PUBLIC SPACES

IN 1519, WHEN HERNÁN CORTÉS and his followers invaded Mexico, many Indian settlements were unplanned huddles of huts. Yet Spanish forces also encountered magnificent and highly organized cities, some with long, straight roads and a central *plaza* fronted by religious buildings. The streets of Cholula, according to Fray Juan de Torquemada, were 'among the best of any city in the world' for width and length. Cortés, in a letter to Charles V, described the great square at Tlatelolco, which was 'twice the size of the town of Salamanca, completely surrounded by arcades, where every day there are more than sixty thousand souls who buy and sell, and where there are all kinds of merchandise from all the provinces ...'. A surviving plan for Tlatelolco's outlying districts, painted around the time of the Conquest, shows approximately four hundred households and gardens, plotted with maximum regularity.

Despite expressions of admiration, Spanish *conquistadores* made haste to demolish these native centres, then implemented building programmes on a massive scale. In 1555 the First Mexican Church Council declared that Indians in remote communities should be persuaded – or compelled, if necessary – to 'congregate in convenient locations and in reasonable towns' where they could be 'instructed in matters necessary for their Salvation'. Separate towns were required for Spanish settlers.

Urban planning in sixteenth-century Mexico was probably influenced by pre-Conquest achievements as well as by the theories of ancient Rome and Renaissance Europe. The result – a systematized grid of broad streets dominated by a central *plaza* with a church and atrium – was far in advance of most Spanish settlements of the period. Building precepts for Mexican towns were exemplified by the Royal Ordinances of 1573. When founding a new settlement, planners were directed to lay out squares, streets and building lots with cords and rods, and to position the main *plaza*, suitably proportioned for celebrations, at the town's heart. For the convenience of traders, *portales* (arcades) were supposed to line this *plaza* and the four main streets diverging from it. Round the *plaza*, land was reserved for the church and for municipal buildings, and also for the shops and dwellings of merchants. Additional legislation sought to regulate the size of *plazas*; in practice, they ranged from 1,860 to 27,800 square metres (20,000 to 300,000 sq. ft). Main streets were approximately 11 metres (35 ft) wide, while the average block, divided into eight plots, covered an area of 32.5 square metres (350 sq. ft).

Opposite *San Miguel Tzinacapan, Puebla* The plaza *(main square) is the focus of village life in Mexico. Here, high in the Sierra de Puebla, a cheerful atmosphere enlivens the yearly market held to mark the festival of San Miguel. Nahua Indians in traditional dress gather in the* plaza *before the* Presidencia *(seat of local government). Beneath white awnings, buyers and sellers gossip and haggle goodnaturedly over prices. The steps provide a resting place. Later, costumed dancers will perform in the* plaza *on behalf of the whole community (see ill. 128).*

Since the colonial era, many towns have expanded at their outer edges, while retaining their original character. Mexico City's main square, which used to incorporate a tree-shaded garden, served as the model for provincial *plazas*. As the hub of community life, these received renewed attention and refurbishment under Porfirio Díaz. Trees and flowers were planted in abundance. Pavilions and bandstands, often of cast iron, were installed: some were oriental and Moorish in inspiration, but others reflected the European fondness for Art Nouveau. Together with iron benches and street lamps, these last were generally imported at great cost from France. Today, most public gardens are carefully tended, and enlivened at weekends by the music of local bands. Handsome public fountains, some dating from the sixteenth century, run with cool water.

Civic monuments, commemorating national leaders and local paragons, take pride of place in many *plazas*. The relationship is indicated by the word *zócalo* (literally 'plinth' or 'base'): applied, by extension, to the capital's main square and its public sculpture, the term is now used for all major squares throughout the Republic. Few monuments show Cortés or the kings of Spain. Most pay tribute to such figures as Cuauhtémoc (the last Aztec emperor), Benito Juárez (revered nineteenth-century president) and Emiliano Zapata (hero of the 1910 Revolution); others celebrate the local deeds of exemplary citizens, or honour generalized virtues such as motherhood and family unity. Styles of representation range from the grandiose to the engagingly modest. Published in 1989, *Mexican Monuments: Strange Encounters* is a treasure trove of bizarre examples. Conceived with humour and affection by environmental sculptor Helen Escobedo, it includes a succession of 'frozen heroes' who tower above the 'pygmied pedestrian'. It also features monuments to tequila, the shrimp and the straw hat, and memorials to such worthy causes as the free textbook, mining and the sewer system.

In the outlying areas of some towns, and in countless villages, the cycle of life is still dominated by agriculture and by rural crafts. Farmers tend their fields in the daytime, sometimes travelling long distances on foot or horseback. Houses may be without running water and electricity. Streets, which are often unpaved, may serve as a working space: in Chiapas, for example, the Tzeltal women of Amatenango del Valle frequently make huge bonfires on the roadway when firing pots. Compulsory communal labour is widespread: under this ancient system, men aged between eighteen and sixty spend a fixed number of days each year on the construction and maintenance of public works.

Most markets take place once a week, on what is commonly referred to as *el día de plaza*. After the Conquest, Indians moved their markets into the newly created squares, often filling adjoining streets with their wares. Awnings of white cotton cloth or brightly coloured plastic sheeting are used by many traders, even in cities. Increasingly, however, open-air stalls are being replaced by purpose-built markets. Some are handsome, well-ventilated constructions, but others resemble breezeblock bunkers and inspire scant affection in the users.

Catholicism is still a vital force in rural Mexico, despite recent inroads by evangelical sects, and most *plazas* are dominated by a colonial church. For administrative and religious purposes, large towns were divided after the Conquest into *barrios* (wards), each with its own chapel and patron saint. On Catholic holidays, worshippers erect floral archways or lay down paths of dyed sawdust and petals outside the church or chapel of their devotion. Holy images are carried through the streets, and serenaded by musicians. Where local dances persist, participants wearing masks and elaborate costumes gather in the main square and join the procession. Often, celebrations are accompanied by rockets and by the burning after dark of a *castillo* – a cane 'castle' made in sections and equipped with fireworks.

On 1 and 2 November, when the souls of the dead are welcomed back on earth, the cemetery is visited by the whole community. Graves are renovated before this festival, although most are carefully tended throughout the year. Frequently embellished with bright paint, glazed tiles and ornamental detail, they may be shaped like miniature houses and churches, or characterized by personal references. In Metepec cemetery, for example, a large marble hat on a marble slab commemorates the sartorial elegance of a local celebrity. Malcolm Lowry, in *Dark as the Grave Wherein my Friend is Laid*, wrote of a vast mausoleum with crypt near Cuernavaca; entirely covered by myriad small mirrors, it reminded him of 'some MGM set for the Ziegfeld Follies'. Other graves, by contrast, are marked by a simple earth mound, a roughly hewn cross and a few petals. In rural Mexico, rich and poor alike share an intimacy with death.

The streets and public squares of rural Mexico are used for trading, working, socializing, relaxing and celebrating. Held in Mexico since pre-Hispanic times, markets include a remarkable range of merchandise. Most take place once a week, attracting people from outlying communities. **95 Papantla, Veracruz** Public building: coloured tiles form geometric motifs. **96 Terrenate, Tlaxcala** Empty, purpose-built market of recent construction; light enters through open spaces in the roof. **97 Yalalag, Oaxaca** Weekly Zapotec market. White awnings of manta (thick cotton cloth), held up by wooden posts, offer protection from the elements. **98 Pahuatlán, Puebla** Goods are displayed on trestle tables or on the ground. Here, maize is spread out on palm mats. **99 San Juan Tlaucingo, Puebla** Families often supplement their income by selling sweets, soft drinks and food to passers-by; the sidewalk outside the home becomes an impromptu restaurant or shop.

95 △

96 △

97△ 98▽

99▽

100△

101△ 102▽

103 △

In towns and villages, the main square is usually dominated by the building for local government. Variously termed the Palacio Municipal, Ayuntamiento or Presidencia, *it generally displays the national emblem of Mexico: an eagle perched on a prickly pear with a serpent in its beak. During national holidays the Mexican flag flies from the flagpole.* **100 Rosario Micaltepec, Oaxaca** *Modest government building, with shuttered windows, in a small pueblo.* **101 Tahmek, Yucatán** *Moorish arches distinguish the portales (arcades) of the Presidencia in this predominantly Maya community.* **102 Ixtlán de Juárez, Oaxaca** *Public buildings are often equipped with Spanish-style portales, where people can rest in the shade or shelter from rain.*

Shops stock a wide variety of goods. Commercial signs and lettering are often hand-painted. **103 Jerez, Zacatecas** *Two-storey building: the balcony is supported by an artificial tree of cement.* **104 Molango, Hidalgo** *The sidewalk becomes an extension of the interior; bags, baskets and hats are offered for sale in the shade of the portales.* **105 Tezontepec, Hidalgo** *Village grocery store painted with Mexico's national emblem. 'La Guadalupana' is a very popular name; it pays homage to the Virgin of Guadalupe, patron saint of Mexico.*

104 △

105 △

106 △

107 △

The needs of the community are often met in ingenious and inexpensive ways. Public spaces are frequently maintained with local labour and local materials. In regions where stone abounds, it is put to numerous uses. **106 Hunucmá, Yucatán** Stone pavement and drain for rainwater.
107 Etla, Oaxaca Opening for the discharge of rainwater. **108 Suchitán, Colima** Cobblestones are often assembled to form flower motifs, starbursts and other decorative patterns. **109 Real del Catorce, San Luis Potosí** Roads and pavements in this mining town were made from local stone. **110 San Pedro y San Pablo Tequixtepec, Oaxaca** A tree is protected round its base with a layer of cobblestones.

The reja (window grille) has been retained in many regions. This ornamental arrangement of metal bars ensures ventilation and security, yet allows contact between house and street. **111 Pinos, Zacatecas** Sidestreet leading to the main square; houses are equipped with window grilles and projecting waterspouts.
112 Xico, Veracruz This photograph shows a group of men from outside the town watching television through the reja. Some householders charge for this privilege.

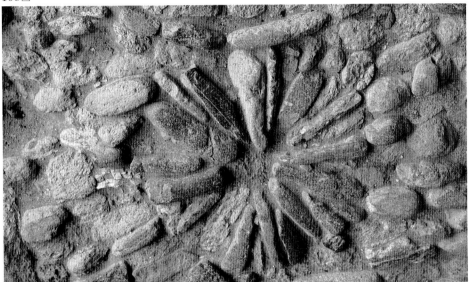

108 △

109 △

110△   111△   112▽

113△ 114▽

In small villages the roadway becomes a working space, maintained by the community at large. Men aged between eighteen and sixty are often required to donate their labour for public works.

113 San Andrés Zautla, Oaxaca Cows and beasts of burden usually spend the night in the security of the solar (yard surrounding the house). Each morning and evening they are led to and from the owner's fields.

114 San Juan Teitipac, Oaxaca In remote communities streets are rarely paved. They are swept before festivals and religious processions; water may be sprinkled on the ground to keep down the dust.

115△ 116▽

115 **San Pablito, Puebla** *Many houses are without running water. Clothes are washed in the village fountain, or in a nearby stream. Here, Otomí women talk companionably while they work. Water for drinking, cooking and personal hygiene is carried home in buckets.* 116 **Los Reyes Metzontla, Puebla** *Pottery is dried in the sun before it is fired; finished pieces are often displayed by the roadside. Here, comales (griddles) lean against an adobe brick wall.*

Spanish-style portales *(arcades) are both decorative and functional. Columns along the front or sides of buildings create a covered walkway where passers-by can seek shelter from sun and rain.*
117 Tlacotalpan, Veracruz *Single-storey buildings fronted by arches are protected by a roof of terracotta tiles.* **118 Tlaxco, Tlaxcala** *Square stone pillars are interspersed with rounded wooden columns on masonry plinths.*

117△ 118▽

119 Alamos, Sonora Cafés and restaurants are often situated under the portales. Even on hot days, clients can sit outside and remain cool. **120 Santa Fe de la Laguna, Michoacán** Introduced into Mexico by Spanish settlers, balconies enable inhabitants to watch the street. Sometimes, as here, they run the whole length of the upper floor. Column capitals, beam ends and railings are decoratively carved from local wood.

119△   120▽

121△   122△   123▽

124△

Ingenious solutions are found for local needs. **121 Temoaya, Mexico State** *Footbridge of wooden poles over a ditch; horizontally positioned sections provide a foothold.* **122 Acxotla del Río, Tlaxcala** *Hanging bridge over a river assembled from wooden planks, metallic cable and rope. It is maintained by community labour.*
123 El Boye, Querétaro *Carefully placed boulders in this dry-laid stone wall serve as steps, enabling children to shorten their journey to and from school.*

Stairs of masonry or concrete often follow hilly and uneven ground. Householders use them as seats to watch the street; on market day passers-by may also use them as a resting place for heavy loads. **124 Olinalá, Guerrero** *Symmetrically arranged steps approach this front door from both sides.*
125 Zumpango del Río, Guerrero *Unintentionally brutalist in style, these steps are made from exposed concrete.*

125△

126△ 127▽

Village streets are the setting for personal joys and griefs, community festivals and children's games. **126 Puerto Azul, Michoacán** Wedding couple and followers returning from the church. **127 Temoaya, Mexico State** Otomí children playing with a homemade cart.

128△   129▽

128 San Miguel Tzinacapan, Puebla
Nahua Indians in the Sierra de Puebla have
retained a number of traditional dances;
these are performed during Catholic
festivals. For the Danza de los Miguelitos
(Dance of the Saint Michaels), villagers
wear finely carved wooden wings and
helmets. Accompanied by musicians, they
wend their way through the streets;
they also perform inside the church.

129 Ihuatzio, Michoacán In Mexico most
parents celebrate their daughter's fifteenth
birthday with a Catholic mass followed by
a party. Here, the cake is being carried
home in two sections from the bakery.

Civic monuments abound in rural Mexico. Some honour national heroes; others commemorate the deeds of local figures. Styles of representation are often endearingly modest and naïve. Monuments are generally situated in the main square, although smaller versions may grace village schools for the edification of pupils.
130 Santiago de Anaya, Hidalgo Detail of a school constructed during the 1930s; walls were decorated freehand with incised designs. The figure in the niche commemorates the anonymous builder with his shovel. **131 Chichimeca, Morelos** School wall painted with the figure of Emiliano Zapata. **132 San Felipe Santiago, Mexico State** L-shaped school: an open corredor runs beneath the overhanging roof. **133 Xocotla, Veracruz** Isolated in lonely splendour, the founder of the local ejido looks out across the town square. **134 Loma Chilar, Oaxaca** A local dignitary, in tie and blazer, watches over the pupils of this primary school.

130 △

131 △

132△   133▽

134▽

135△   136△   137▽

138△

Mexicans work extremely hard throughout the year. In rural areas, where entertainments are few, festivals and fairs offer respite from agricultural and domestic labour. Introduced into Mexico by Spanish settlers, bullfighting remains popular in many regions. **135 Hunucmá, Yucatán** Although some bullrings are permanent constructions, others are temporary structures of poles and wattle secured with twine. When the fair is over, they are rapidly disassembled. The poles can be re-used, but the wattle is discarded. **136 and 137 San Lucas, Michoacán** Here villagers rest their structure on an existing stone wall. **138 Tlaxcala City** Solidly built with stone walls and terracotta roof-tiles, this bullring was inaugurated in 1880. **139 Hunucmá, Yucatán** Travelling funfairs are a popular form of entertainment. Roundabouts, stalls and sideshows are set up in the main square. Seen here are Maya women with embroidered skirts and huipiles (tunics).

139△

In many towns and villages the main square serves as a public garden.
140 Tzintzuntzan, Michoacán Carved lion of pale pink stone. Statues – small or large, modest or sophisticated – are a feature of many parks. **141 Alamos, Sonora** The quiosco (bandstand) is usually positioned in the centre of the park. On Sundays and public holidays visitors are serenaded by the local brass band. **142 Lagos de Moreno, Guanajuato** Trees and flowering plants are carefully tended; topiary is practised in some towns. **143 Jerez, Zacatecas** Quiosco roof: inspired by French designs, this elegant construction of cast iron dates from the Porfirian era.
144 Contla, Puebla Twentieth-century quiosco erected by local builders; its massive proportions give it the air of a fortified tower. **145 Jerez, Zacatecas** Porfirian-style, white-painted benches of cast iron.

140 △

141 △

142 △

143△ 144▽ 145▽

146△ 147△ 148▽

149 △

Despite the proselytism of countless evangelical sects, Catholic faith is still a dominant force in Mexico. Shrines by the side of country roads and village streets are a tangible reminder of religious devotion.
146 **San Pedro Coyutla, Veracruz** *Thatched bell-tower on wooden stilts; the bellringer climbs the notched ladder.*
147 **Tlamanca, Puebla** *Whitewashed shrine on top of a hill.* 148 **Santiaguito, Oaxaca** *Shrine with cross shaded by a laurel tree near the village church.* 149 **Tenzontla, Jalisco** *Shrine, embedded in a stone wall, for the Santo Niño de Atocha.* 150 **San Pedro Mártir, Oaxaca** *Street shrine: Zapotec villagers leave flowers and small offerings to adorn the holy cross.* 151 **Los Reyes Metzontla, Puebla** *A street-corner shrine safeguards the well-being of local families; in some communities each* barrio *has its own shrine.*

150 △

151 △

152△ 153▽

Indian and mestizo villagers visit the local church to share in public expressions of devotion, or for private contemplation and prayer. Many buildings are centuries old.
152 Contla, Puebla *An undulating wall of stuccoed masonry encloses the church atrium.* **153 Mitla, Oaxaca** *A stone angel guards the entrance to the church.*

154△ 155▽

154 Tlalixtac de Cabrera, Oaxaca
Covered gateway leading to the atrium;
an altar is embedded in the wall.
155 Yolotepec, Hidalgo Atrium wall of
thick masonry; the merlons along the top
are typical of this region.

123

156 **Yolotepec, Hidalgo** Massive stone buttresses support the walls of the church.
157 *San Andrés Tenejapa, Veracruz* Villagers in many regions construct handsome archways using the sotol palm, fresh flowers and other elements. These serve to decorate the church during religious festivals.

156△ 157▽

158 *Cosoleacaque, Veracruz Church altar with saints.* **159** *Matlatengo, Hidalgo Village church with a hip roof of tiles. Suspended under the eaves, the bells are rung with the aid of a long rope.*

158△ 159▽

160△ 161▽

Builders of rural churches often drew their inspiration from the ecclesiastical architecture of cities. Forms and imagery were adapted to express the sensibility of local people. **160 Teotlancingo, Puebla** In this region Baroque styles were interpreted through a profusion of tiles and plaster decoration. **161 Izúcar de Matamoros, Puebla** Interior pilaster adorned by a small angel.

162△   163▽

162 *Macuilxochitl, Oaxaca* The massive
scale of these columns contrasts with
the diminutive size of the font.
163 *Jonacatepec, Morelos* Richly decorated
columns and guitar-playing mermaids in
Baroque style embellish the façade of the
church of San Martín.

The cemetery is often located next to the church. Some tombs are complex structures that reflect the wealth of the family (see p. 194); other graves, by contrast, are marked by little more than a wooden cross and a handwritten board.   **164 Tenzontla, Jalisco** Tomb in the shape of a house. **165 Mina, Nuevo León** Cemetery gateway.   **166 Lachigolo, Oaxaca** Cemetery gateway set in a wall of adobe bricks.   **167 Jalcomulco, Puebla** Tombs in the shape of chapels.   **168 Tecominoacán, Tabasco** Miniature churches and houses, grouped as in a village, mark the graves of the dead.

164 △

165 △

166△ 167▽

168▽

4

THE HACIENDA

'THIS IS A FINE WILD SCENE. The house stands entirely alone; not a tree near it. Great mountains rise behind it, and in every other direction, as far as the eye can see, are vast plains, over which the wind comes whistling fresh and free, with nothing to impede its triumphant progress. In front of the house is a clear sheet of water, a great deep square basin for collecting the rain. These *jagueys*, as they are called, are very common in Mexico, where there are few rivers, and where the use of machines for raising water is by no means general as yet. There is no garden here, but there are a few shrubs and flowers in the inner courtyard. The house inside is handsome, with a chapel and a patio, which is occasionally used as a plaza de toros. The rooms are well fitted up, and the bedroom walls covered with a pretty French paper, representing scenes of Swiss rural life. There are great outhouses, stables for the mules and horses, and stone barns for the wheat and barley, which, together with the pulque, form the produce of this hacienda.'

The country estate of Tepenacasco, described here by Frances Calderón de la Barca in May 1840, lay 'a few leagues from Tulancingo' in the state of Hidalgo. It was one of several owned by the same wealthy family. Their *haciendas*, in common with many others, were suffering the ill-effects of political instability. The Wars for Independence (1810–21) had brought an end to Spanish rule, but they had also ushered in a long period of turbulence. Between May 1833 and August 1855 the presidency changed hands thirty-six times; bandits infested the highways, and would often rob *haciendas*. While in Mexico, Frances Calderón de la Barca saw 'ruins everywhere – here a viceroy's country palace serving as a tavern . . . – there, a whole village crumbling to pieces; roofless houses, broken down walls and arches, an old church – the remains of a convent . . .'.

Forty-one years later, in the summer of 1881, the *hacienda* of Tepenacasco was visited by another foreign traveller, Thomas Unett Brocklehurst. Order and optimism had largely replaced chaos during the presidencies of Benito Juárez and Sebastián Lerdo de Tejada; Porfirio Díaz, who took power in 1876, promised progress and the rule of law. Brocklehurst saw a bright future for Mexico, 'this latterly much distracted and suffering country'. His detailed description of Tepenacasco, quoted in the Introduction, offers an up-dated vision of a prosperous, well-irrigated and apparently enlarged *hacienda*.

During the second half of the nineteenth century, innumerable *haciendas* were similarly modernized or totally rebuilt, often on a very grand scale. This process

Opposite *San Bartolomé del Monte, Calpulalpan, Tlaxcala* Most haciendas *extended over vast areas; at their heart was the big house. During the nineteenth century some houses were enlarged or re-modelled, while others were built from scratch. Styles were freely borrowed from other lands and other periods. Stone lions guard the wrought-iron gateway of this once thriving* hacienda. Pulque, *its chief source of revenue in Porfirian times, is still produced here, though on a smaller scale than formerly.*

of renovation and expansion was not new. Throughout their history, Mexico's rural estates had evolved continuously to reflect the political, economic and technological changes of the age. Over centuries, as fortunes waxed and waned, buildings were modified and boundaries redrawn by the founding families or by a succession of owners. It was under Porfirio Díaz, however, that many *haciendas* experienced their most prosperous phase. Agrarian rebellions and social unrest were ruthlessly quashed; lawlessness and brigandage were kept in check by the *rurales* (rural police forces), while the rapid spread of the railways facilitated the transport of merchandise even through mountainous and broken terrain. It was during this time of economic growth and stability that most of the *haciendas* represented here achieved their maximum splendour.

Although some estates operated with a comparatively modest acreage, others rivalled Belgium or Holland in size. Production varied in accordance with the climate and terrain. The grain *haciendas* of central Mexico supplied city-dwellers with maize and wheat; additional crops included barley, beans and chiles. *Pulque*, described by Brocklehurst as 'the national beverage of the country', brought affluence to landowners in the states of Hidalgo, Mexico and Tlaxcala. In Yucatán, wealth was generated through the cultivation and export of *henequén*, or sisal. Sugarcane plantations were located where water is plentiful in the *tierra caliente* (hot lands) of Veracruz, Michoacán, Morelos, lowland Puebla and the Autlán region of Jalisco. Other tropical estates yielded tobacco, coffee, fruit, *cacao*, vanilla, rubber, brazilwood, mahogany, indigo and cotton. Cattle, horses, goats and sheep were raised in vast numbers on livestock *haciendas* in northern Mexico. Some landowners in the mountainous areas of Zacatecas, San Luis Potosí, Durango, Guanajuato and Hidalgo were fortunate enough to own silver mines, where ore was extracted and refined.

Many *haciendas* were extremely isolated, as the writings of European travellers stress. Frances Calderón de la Barca described San Nicolás, a sugarcane *hacienda* near Izúcar de Matamoros, as 'one of the finest estates in the republic', yet she found her visit there a cheerless experience. 'There is a feeling of vastness, of solitude, and of dreariness in some of these great haciendas, which is oppressive. Especially about noon, when everything is still, and there is no sound except the incessant buzz of myriads of insects, I can imagine it like what the world must have been before man was created.'

Predictably, most wealthy landowners preferred life in the cities. They paid short visits to their estates, but entrusted the day-to-day running to administrators, who kept the accounts and supervised the workforce. To make up for their isolation, many *haciendas* were almost totally self-sufficient, variously incorporating brick-kilns, stone quarries, weaving sheds, workshops for blacksmiths and carpenters, dairies, beehives, orchards, tanneries, cattle-pens, stables and threshing floors. Grain was stored in immense barns, many dating from the colonial period. Specialist work areas included the *tinacal* (*pulque*-making hall), sugar mills, buildings with yards for smelting ore, and processing plants for *henequén*. Aqueducts, dams and reservoirs kept estates supplied with water. Defensive measures included high perimeter walls and observation towers. One *hacienda* visited by Brocklehurst near Pachuca had 'fortified gates, more fitted for a small town than a single farm'.

At the heart of the *casco*, or *hacienda* complex, stood the chapel and the big house, where wealth could be openly displayed. Building work rarely involved academically trained architects. In some colonial houses the original features remained dominant, but more fanciful dwellings drew inspiration from other lands and other ages. Many owners, fired perhaps by trips to Europe, opted for French-style *châteaux*, Italianate *palazzos*, Renaissance villas or Victorian Gothic mansions; others chose instead to incorporate Moorish or Indian elements. Spacious and comfortable interiors also reflected imported fashions, while patios and gardens, filled with flowers and foliage, offered landowners and their guests an outdoor escape from the working life of the *hacienda*.

No such respite was available to the peons, however. On many estates, debts, caused by low wages, forced them to remain as virtual slaves, labouring from dawn until dusk. While visiting the *pulque hacienda* of powerful bankers, Brocklehurst asked to see the workers' cottages. These were situated 'in lines beyond the farm buildings. Each family, large or small, had a room some sixteen feet square, which seemed to be equally shared in by the family, the poultry, and the pig.' Oppression and social injustice were to lead eventually to the 1910 Revolution, the redistribution of land, and the demise of the *hacienda* system.

169 △

Many haciendas *resembled fortresses, with look-out towers, high crenellated walls, gun-slots, grilled windows and studded doors.* **169 San Isidro, Hidalgo** *Completed in 1914, this imposing* hacienda *rises like a medieval European castle amid a mass of* magueyes *and* nopales. **170 San Bartolomé del Monte, Calpulalpan, Tlaxcala** *Stone lions and heraldic devices served as symbols of status (see also p. 130).* **171 San Bartolomé del Monte, Calpulalpan, Tlaxcala** *A richly ornamented look-out tower is situated at each of the four corners of the* hacienda's *outer wall.* **172 Santa Inés Tepozintla, Tlaxcala** *Look-out tower with gun-slots and a stone balustrade.* **173 Tecajete, Hidalgo** *A bell hangs over the entrance to this elegant* pulque hacienda. *Windows and gun-slots have been decoratively outlined with black paint.*

170 △

171△

172△　173▽

174△　175▽

176▽

174 *San Antonio Millet, Yucatán* Set in parkland in the English manner, this palatial residence combines several different styles of architecture.   175 **Virreyes, Puebla** *Agricultural* hacienda *showing Moorish influence. The door is decoratively carved with geometric motifs; small grilled windows are set in thick walls.*   176 **Xala, Mexico State** *Cattle* hacienda. *Completed in 1785, the residence shows oriental influence.*   177 **Tlalayote, Hidalgo** *Gothic-style portico. In the distance is the* tienda de raya *(estate shop).*   178 **San Antonio Chautla, Puebla** *Artificial lake with a house for guests. Inspired by romantic European palaces, this* hacienda *is chiefly known today as an idyllic location for films and television commercials.*

177 △

178 △

179 △

Lions were unknown in Mexico until knowledge of them was brought over after the Conquest by Spanish settlers. The king of the beasts was symbolically used to guard many eighteenth- and nineteenth-century haciendas, *giving owners a feeling of strength and power.* **179 Chenché de las Torres, Yucatán** Stone lion on an henequén hacienda. **180 Majoma, Zacatecas** Door-knocker in the shape of a lion's head.

Even in hot and arid regions, most haciendas *had shady spaces and luxuriant foliage. The big house was usually built around several interior patios; sometimes a veranda overlooked a verdant garden.* **181 San Lorenzo, Parras, Coahuila** *Sunlight shines through the massive masonry railings of a covered walkway.* **182 San Andrés, Mexico State** *Veranda lined with potted plants.* **183 Mazaquiahuac, Tlaxcala** *Painted panel with peacocks. Often, hacendados kept live peacocks in their gardens.*

180 △

181△   182▽   183▽

As in Moorish courtyards, the play of water in a central fountain suggested coolness in hot weather. Ornamental sculpture, predominantly French in style, gained popularity from the mid-nineteenth century. Most patios have fallen into disrepair or become overgrown, yet they retain an aura of repose. **184 Exquitlan, Tulancingo, Hidalgo** Cinderella and the prince, painted in the style of the Pre-Raphaelites on a panel on a courtyard wall. **185 San Mateo Ixtlahuaca, Hidalgo** A raised veranda encloses the courtyard on all four sides. In the fountain, two stone dolphins serve as waterspouts.

184△　185▽

186 Exquitlan, Tulancingo, Hidalgo
*Fountain with stone cupid; the painted
panel behind is shown in ill. 184.*
187 Bocas, San Luis Potosí *An open
corredor surrounds the patio. As in colonial
times, wide arches are supported by
massive masonry columns.*

186△   187▽

188△ 189▽

190▽

191 △

192 △

Many hacienda *interiors have fallen into disrepair, or been modernized by recent inhabitants. A few retain their original features, however.* **188** *San Antonio Tochatlaco, Hidalgo Tiled kitchen with a charcoal-burning stove. Cooking utensils of copper and glazed pottery line the walls.* **189** *Chimalpa, Hidalgo Dining room with wood panelling. Imported European tea and dinner services are displayed in the cabinet. The long table is illuminated by a gas lamp.* **190** *San Antonio Ometusco, Mexico State English hunting scenes adorn the walls of the big house.* **191** *San Miguel la Blanca, Puebla Window blind showing a palace with oriental features surrounded by lush vegetation.* **192** *Asunción, Querétaro English-style garden and woodland where hacendados and their guests could stroll and take the air.* **193** *Ocotepec, Hidalgo Bedroom equipped with heavy wooden furniture. The washbasin and water jug are of fine china. Walls are decorated with imported floral wallpaper.*

193 △

143

194△

195△ 196▽

197 △

Most estates were entrusted to an administrator. The office was usually situated on the ground floor of the big house, to one side of the main entrance. By the end of the Porfirian era, most offices were equipped with the latest technology. **194 Carmona, Mexico State** Postbox decorated with a lion on the outer wall of the office; letters were pushed through a narrow slit in the mouth. **195 Tepechichilco, Hidalgo** Pay-window of wood. At the end of each week, the peones *would line up to receive money or tokens; these they exchanged for goods in the* tienda de raya. **196 Santa María Tochatlaco, Hidalgo** Hacienda *office with desks for clerks.*

During the eighteenth and nineteenth centuries, haciendas *became increasingly self-sufficient; isolated as they were, they made every effort to provide for their own needs. For the* peones, *the work was onerous and the hours were long; many were forced by low wages to contract debts, which bound them to the* haciendas *for the rest of their lives.* **197 San Antonio Tochatlaco, Hidalgo** *This erstwhile* tienda de raya *is now run as a normal shop. Stocks include bottled drinks, sweets and batteries.* **198 Carmona, Mexico State** Tienda de raya: *here peons exchanged wages or tokens for basic necessities such as flour, sugar and cloth.* **199 San Antonio Techalote, Tlaxcala** *During the Porfirian era, many* haciendas *were linked by rail to the local railway station. This private carriage displays the name of the* hacienda.

198 △

HACIENDA SAN ANTONIO

199 △

200△ 201▽

Within the encomienda system, which preceded the rise of the great haciendas, groups of Indians were entrusted to Spanish settlers, who commanded their labour and exacted tribute in exchange for religious instruction. Hacendados, too, were responsible for the spiritual welfare of their peons. **200 San Antonio Ometusco, Mexico State** This pulque hacienda resembled a small town in size and organization. Built with stones and bricks, and adorned with English tiles, the capilla (chapel) achieved majestic proportions. **201 Magueyitos, Veracruz** Polychrome wooden statue of a saint attired in silk brocade. Chapels displayed images of the Virgin Mary and the patron saint of the hacienda.

202△ 203▽

202 Santa Inés Tepozintla, Tlaxcala
*Chapel built during the eighteenth century
and restored during the nineteenth century.
Some chapels stand apart; others are
incorporated into the main building, as
here.* **203 Yaxcopoil, Yucatán** *Altar in
neo-Gothic style from the Porfirian era.*

147

204 △

The wealth of each hacienda depended on its produce. On large estates, barns and outhouses attained colossal proportions. **204 Xala, Mexico State** *Barn with massive stone walls and stout wooden beams; tall columns support the roof. Flared window openings allow light to penetrate and air to circulate.* **205 San Nicolás el Grande, Tlaxcala** *Eighteenth-century stone granary for storing barley. The bell on the roof could be used to summon the peons to work or to sound the alarm.* **206 Espejel, Hidalgo** *Granary with decorative turrets in the Dutch style. Strips of corrugated iron replace the original roof.*

207 Chavarría, Hidalgo *Landowners rarely lived on their estates. Instead, they entrusted the management to overseers, whose houses were relatively comfortable. These nineteenth-century examples in neo-Gothic style were built beside the chapel.* **208 Villa de Teyontepec, Hidalgo** *One-room dwellings of stone with adjoining kitchens. Peons lived here with their wives and children.* **209 Tetlapayac, Hidalgo** *Peons' houses of brick and stone: roofs are tiled.*

205 △

206 △

207△ 208▽

209▽

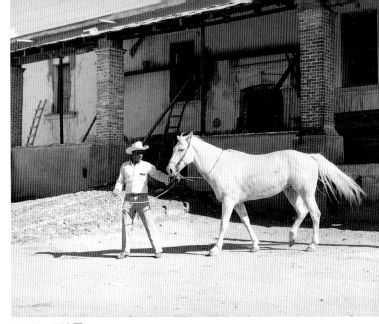

210△   211△ 212▽

213 △

214 △

Horses and cattle were introduced into the
New World by Spanish settlers. In Mexico
charrería (horsemanship) soon became an
important part of life on the great estates.
210 San Miguel Ometusco, Hidalgo Cattle
crossing the patio de trabajo (working
courtyard). The surrounding walls were
fortified in the manner of battlements.
211 Chavarría, Hidalgo Horses, mules and
burros still play an important role on
working haciendas.   **212 Bocas, San Luis
Potosí** An archway marks the entrance to
the stables. The massive walls are of
masonry. By the late eighteenth century
Bocas had become an hacienda ganadera
dedicated to sheep-rearing for the textile
industry. Maize production was also
substantial.

   213 Bolaños, Jalisco The outer walls of
haciendas were often equipped with look-
out towers. Shown here is the entrance to
one such tower.   **214 Rincón Umbroso,
San Luis Potosí** Stone gateway to the
stables: horizontal wooden bars were
slotted into holes. The wall is buttressed by
a conical support.   **215 Soltepec, Tlaxcala**
Colonial aqueduct of local stone.
216 Malpaís, Hidalgo Underground water
channels served to irrigate the land.
217 Soltepec, Tlaxcala Outer wall with
merlons. Medieval-style towers with gun-
slots flank the main entrance.

215 △

216 △

217 △

218 *San Antonio Ometusco, Mexico State* Twin granaries divided by a road. Working areas were kept away from the big house, so that the inhabitants would not be disturbed by noise or unpleasant smells.
219 *San Miguel Hueyapan, Mexico State* Two-storey kiln for firing bricks. Made from bricks, it serviced the building needs of the hacienda. **220** *Rincón Umbroso,* **San Luis Potosí** Windowless granary from the colonial era, with waterspouts and a flat roof for drying maize. The stone walls are thickly plastered. **221** *San Miguel* **Regla, Hidalgo** Eighteenth-century chimneys for smelting silver on a mining hacienda. **222** *La Peña, Zacatecas* Barn made from adobe bricks and stone. Wheat was stored high up, with an airhole to ensure ventilation.

218△

219△

220△   221▽   222▽

223 △

224 △ 225 ▽

226△

During the nineteenth century, the economy of Yucatán was linked to the production and export of henequén *for the manufacture of rope and twine. In recent decades the rise of synthetic fibre has eclipsed the demand for* henequén, *yet crops are still grown in many places.*
223 Yucatán Henequén *plants.*
224 Dzoyaché, Yucatán *Processing plant: here* henequén *spikes are scraped to separate the pulp from the fibres.*
225 Dzoyaché Yucatán *Mound of newly processed* henequén *fibres.*
  Many haciendas *depended on the production of* pulque.   **226 Tepechichilco, Hidalgo** *The pulque-making hall (tinacal) of a working hacienda. Peones used to collect their wages from the pay-booth.* **227 Totoapa, Hidalgo** *Maguey plants are tended by the* tlachiquero. *The sweet sap (aguamiel) is extracted by means of a long gourd (acocote).*

227△

Landowners and their families were often laid to rest in their own graveyard adjoining the hacienda. **228 Parras, Coahuila** Ornate tombs of the Porfirian era. **229 Mazaquiahuac, Tlaxcala** Private cemetery overrun by weeds.

228△　229▽

The disintegration of Mexico's haciendas began with the 1910 Revolution, and ended with the redistribution of land during the Agrarian Reform. Many hacienda *buildings* were destroyed by revolutionaries or left to decay by their owners. **230 *San Antonio Coahuixtla, Morelos*** Crumbling trapiche, or sugar mill. **231 *San Martín Rinconada, Puebla*** Ruined hacienda church.

230△ 231▽

5

TOWN RESIDENCES

DURING THE COLONIAL PERIOD, immense wealth and power were concentrated in the capital of New Spain (Spanish Mexico). Magnificent churches, convents, monasteries, hospitals, government buildings and palatial residences, erected on the Aztec ruins of Tenochtitlan, reflected rising fortunes and changing fashions. Thomas Gage, an English friar, was a visitor there in 1625; later he recorded his impressions of 'one of the richest cities in the world'. By his account, 'all the Indians far and near are subdued, ... consequently all arms are forgotten, and the Spaniards live so secure from enemies that there is neither gate, wall, bulwark, platform, tower, armory, ammunition, or ordinance to secure and defend the city from a domestic or foreign enemy.'

Most sixteenth-century buildings had been functional and fortress-like, but the Baroque age was characterized by conspicuous consumption and by a love of ornamentation. Gage's descriptions evoke the period. He pronounced the capital's churches 'the fairest that ever my eyes beheld. The roofs and beams are in many of them all daubed with gold. Many altars have sundry marble pillars, and others are decorated with brazil-wood stays standing one above another with tabernacles for several saints richly wrought in golden colours, so that twenty thousand ducats is a common price of many of them.' Streets were praised for their 'breadth and cleanness', and for 'the riches of the shops which do adorn them'. Worthy of special note was 'La Platería, or Goldsmiths' Street, where a man's eyes may behold in less than an hour many millions' worth of gold, silver, pearls and jewels'.

Opulent colonists lived in fashionable enclaves: 'For stately buildings the street called *del Aguila*, the Street of the Eagle, exceeds the rest. There live gentlemen, and courtiers, and judges belonging to the Chancery, and there is the palace of the Marqués del Valle from the line of Hernando Cortés.' The houses of wealthy Spaniards were 'very fair and spacious' with 'gardens of recreation' and interior patios. 'Their buildings are with stone and brick very strong, but not high, by reason of the many earthquakes ...'. Humidity and flooding were additional problems in the capital, for 'water hath its passage under all the streets of it'.

Foreign travellers of the eighteenth and early nineteenth centuries were similarly struck by the magnificence of the capital – described by Baron von Humboldt as 'the City of Palaces' – and by the beauty of other centres such as Puebla de los Angeles, Valladolid (now Morelia) and Oaxaca. Underlying the great fortunes of the era were the manufacturing industries, commerce and mining.

Opposite *Mexico City* Wealthy town house, photographed at the turn of the century. The Porfirian era was one of industrial expansion. While the living conditions of the urban poor deteriorated, the rich became richer. In the capital, broad boulevards were opened and palatial homes constructed in fashionable residential areas. Building styles were largely borrowed from Europe. Here, elements reveal neo-classical, neo-Gothic and Victorian romanesque inspiration.

Vast sums of money were invested in the purchase and upkeep of rural estates, and in the building or reconstruction of grand city dwellings. Prominent families included the Condes del Valle de Orizaba, the Condes de Heras y Soto and the Condes de Santiago de Calimaya (see pages 162–5). The assets amassed by the first Conde de Santa María de Regla became legendary. Born Pedro Romero de Terreros in Andalusia in 1710, he settled in New Spain and inherited considerable riches from his brother and his uncle; the Veta Vizcaína mine at Real del Monte, left to him by a friend, made him the wealthiest man in the land. When his son was christened, according to Frances Calderón de la Barca, 'the whole party walked from his house to the church upon ingots of silver'. Intent on establishing a noble family, he purchased titles for himself and his sons, and a host of *haciendas*. The entrance to his two-storey residence in Mexico City, built from soft, red *tezontle* stone, is shown on page 165.

The Wars for Independence were followed by political instability, yet visitors to the new republic found the capital to be a place of glittering balls, fine carriages and European fashions. In 1840 Frances Calderón de la Barca rented a residence in 'one of the noblest-looking cities in the world': 'It is a handsome new house, built by General G—, and has the fault of being only too large. Built in a square, like all Mexican houses, the ground-floor, which has a stone-paved court with a fountain in the middle, contains about twenty rooms, besides outhouses, coach-houses, stables, pigeon-house, garden-house, etc. The second storey where the principal apartments are, the first-floor being chiefly occupied by servants, has the same number of rooms, with coal-room, wood-room, bath-room, and water everywhere, in the court below, in the garden, and on the azotea [flat roof], which is very spacious, and where, were the house our house, we might build a *mirador* [belvedere], and otherwise ornament it . . .'.

As the wife of the Foreign Minister for Spain, Frances Calderón de la Barca was welcomed into the homes of the wealthy and powerful. In 1840 she visited the Countess C—, 'who has a magnificent house, with suites of large rooms, of which the drawing room is particularly handsome, of immense size, the walls beautifully painted, the subjects religious, and where I found one of Broadwood's finest grand pianos.' This mansion, with its 'cabinets inlaid with gold, fine paintings, and hundreds of rich and curious things', and the one adjoining, which also belonged to the family, were 'palaces in vastness'.

In major cities outside the capital, the residences of weathy landowners could achieve similar splendour. While searching for ancient Maya remains in 1840, John L. Stephens visited don Simón Peón, 'the proprietor of the ruins of Uxmal'. His house in Mérida was 'a large aristocratic-looking mansion of dark gray stone, with balconied windows, occupying nearly the half of one side of the plaza'. This was the family's town residence, 'the different members of it having separate haciendas'. In the City of Puebla, Frances Calderón de la Barca was invited to a house that she thought 'more elegantly furnished than any in Mexico. It is of immense size, and the floors beautifully painted. One large room is furnished with pale blue satin, another with crimson damask, and there are fine inlaid tables, handsome mirrors, and everything in very good taste.'

The Porfirian era created new fortunes, and fostered the rise of new residential areas in the capital. Imposing, eclectically designed villas were built by landowners and industrialists in the fashionable *colonias* of Santa María la Ribera, Juárez, Roma and Condesa. Wide boulevards, elegant shops and fine restaurants impressed foreign observers, and reminded Thomas Unett Brockle-hurst of Paris. After dark, the wealthy attended supper parties and music recitals, gambled, or went to the theatre. The Casino Español (see page 169) was the scene of numerous balls, including one held for Porfirio Díaz in 1910: surrounded by nine thousand light bulbs, guests dined in splendour and waltzed to music from *The Merry Widow*.

At the same time, foreign writers could not ignore the opposition between prosperity and acute poverty, elegance and squalor, that defined urban life. Conditions in the lower-class *barrios* were deplorable. Carl Sartorius was echoing many earlier observers, and foreshadowing later ones, when he noted in 1858: 'The Mexican population presents the most striking contrasts, unlike that of any city in north-western Europe. On one side splendour and luxury, elegant carriages, and Parisian toilette, on the other dirt and indifference . . .'.

These details are taken from a splendid
colonial mansion in **Mexico City** that was
the city residence of the Condes del Valle
de Orizaba, owners of sugar-cane haciendas
in the state of Veracruz. Originally built in
the sixteenth century, it was reconstructed
and elaborately decorated in Baroque style
during the eighteenth century. Popularly
known as the House of Tiles, it is situated
on the calle de Madero, where it now
operates as a shop and restaurant.
232 The façade is decorated in Poblano
style with distinctive blue and white glazed
tiles.   **233** Baroque mirror-frame of carved
wood.

232△   233▽

234 *Exterior stone pilasters feature a wealth of intricate carving.* 235 *Two storeys high, the building incorporates a patio surrounded by* corredores. *The flat roof is equipped with stone* cañones *(waterspouts). Stone railings and columns are richly carved.*

234△   235▽

236△ 237▽

238▽

Ornamental details carved in stone were an integral part of Baroque architecture in **Mexico City**. 236 An elaborate and highly decorative façade of carved stone distinguishes the eighteenth-century church of San Felipe. 237 Stone lions flank the main staircase in the erstwhile residence of the Condes de Santiago de Calimaya on Pino Suárez. Rebuilt in 1779 by Francisco Guerrero y Torres, this magnificent mansion is now the Mexico City Museum (see Introduction). 238 Shell-shaped fountain with a guitar-playing mermaid in the palace of the Condes de Santiago de Calimaya. 239 Detail of an eighteenth-century door from the mansion of the Condes de Heras y Soto. 240 House owned by the wealthy hacendado Pedro Romero de Terreros, the first Conde de Santa María de Regla. Born in Spain in 1710, he died in Mexico in 1781. The doors are embellished with bossed nail heads.

239 △

240 △

241△ 242▽

Nineteenth-century residences in **Mexico City** incorporated a wide range of architectural styles and reflected the wealth of their owners. **241** Moorish tower with horseshoe arches. The ornamentation of the balustrade recalls Greek and Roman models featuring honeysuckle flowers and leaves. **242** Façade in early Renaissance style. Roman in inspiration, the arch has a carved keystone with a Greek theme; the side pilasters are characteristic of neo-classical architecture.

243△ 244▽

243 *Residence in florid English, or Tudor style. Renaissance elements include the heavy masonry decoration surrounding the windows of the middle storey. Eclectic urban architecture of this period aspired to be imposing and grand, but was frequently inelegant and over-ornate.* 244 *House built in Renaissance style. Columns and cornices emulate Greek architecture. The balustrade is classically conceived, while the funerary urns along the top are neo-classical elements.*

167

245 Puebla City *Elegant street lamp of cast iron from the turn of the century, inspired by French Art Nouveau styles.*
246 Mexico City *Moorish pavilion, with a structure of cast iron, designed by José M. de Ibarrola. Exhibited in New Orleans 1884–5, it was brought back to Mexico and re-erected in the Alameda central, then moved in 1900 to the Alameda de Santa María la Ribera.*

245 △   246 ▽

247 Mexico City *The Casino Español, built between 1901 and 1903 on Isabel la Católica, catered for the wealthiest residents of Spanish descent in the capital. It boasted an ornate and costly ballroom and banqueting hall.* **248 Mexico City** *Stained-glass windows were a feature of the great hall of the Casino Español.*

247△   248▽

249 △

250 △

During the Porfirian era, the homes of the wealthy were replete with ornamentation inspired by French architectural models.
249 Mexico City *Detail of a house interior, with decorative plaster mouldings featuring flower and leaf motifs.*
250 Pachuca, Hidalgo *A finely carved wooden door marks the entrance to the Casa Cravioto. The owner, General Cravioto, was a powerful* hacendado.
251 Pachuca, Hidalgo *Urn of cast metal and wrought-iron railing, from the Casa Cravioto.* **252 Puebla City** *Balcony of carved stone.* **253 Mexico City** *Ground-floor window with a grille of wrought iron.* **254 Mexico City** *Oval window elegantly framed with fruit and leaves of carved stone.*

251 △

252△ 253▽   254▽

255△   256△   257▽

258△

Born in Cambourne in Cornwall, Francisco Rule settled in **Pachuca, Hidalgo**, and became the owner of a mining hacienda. His residence, completed in 1896, reflected prevailing fashions of the period.
255 *Lamp illuminating the central staircase.* 256 *Door incorporating glass panels etched with floral motifs and the initials 'F.R.'* 257 *Corredor overlooking the central patio.* 258 *Façade: window decorations in stained glass included the initials of the owner.* 259 *Imported wallpaper.*

259△

The wealthy were often laid to rest in considerable splendour. **260 Mexico City** Public figures were frequently interred in the cemetery of San Fernando Rey. After the burial of President Benito Juárez in 1872, however, this famous graveyard was closed. **261 Mexico City** Burial plaque in the cemetery of San Fernando Rey: a powerful *hacendado commemorates the death of his son at twenty-five days.*

EL NIÑO CARLOS
DE LANDA Y ESCANDON
DE 25 DIAS:
MARZO 15 DE 1853

26

262△ 263▽

262 **Parras, Coahuila** *Wealthy section of the town cemetery.* 263 **Mexico City** *Elegant family tombs in the cemetery of San Fernando Rey.*

6

THE UNCOMMON TOUCH

FOR ANDRÉ BRETON in the 1930s, Mexico was 'the Surrealist place *par excellence*' with a long tradition of the marvellous. He was awed by Mexico's 'millennial roots', intrigued by the unexpected juxtapositions that he saw within everyday life, and full of admiration for Mexico's popular arts, which have retained their vitality to the present day.

Vernacular architecture, too, can surprise the onlooker, by presenting uncommon solutions to practical problems. Houses of agave or rye stalks may appear 'exotic' or 'quaint' to the outsider, yet they are functional constructions which have evolved over time to suit local requirements. Ingenious examples of non-industrial technology include a brick-kiln elegantly formed by the bricks to be fired, and a water-tower with a ramp for mules. Sophisticated urban architecture relies increasingly on prefabrication and on the creation of flexible and movable structures, yet many of the 'rustic' houses and granaries in Part 2 fulfil these same aims, as do the partially reusable bullrings on page 116. The recycling of diverse and often unlikely elements is widespread in Mexico: it seems logical to make use of a pre-Hispanic stone carving in a contemporary house, but few towns have an entire bus set into a wall, as may be seen in Santiaquillo, Zacatecas (page 198).

Popular architecture often reveals a deep-rooted love of ornament. The historical precedents are many and varied. As described in the Introduction, pre-Conquest buildings were frequently embellished with non-functional elements of stone and stucco. In the Puuc region, Maya buildings were characterized by high roof-combs, decorative columns, finials, lattice-work motifs, masks and fantastic serpents executed with a strong feeling for balance and harmony. During the twentieth century, many architects and designers have borrowed from pre-Hispanic cultures. *The Mayan Revival Style* (1984), by Marjorie Ingle, affectionately documents the 'exotic' influence of the Maya, the Mixtec, the Toltec and the Aztec on North American buildings of the Art Deco period. In modern Mexico, hotels and restaurants sometimes exhibit 'pre-Hispanic' features, garishly recreated in painted polystyrene. The aims of the late Salazar Monroy (author, inventor and antiquarian) were altogether more exalted when he planned his ambitious complex at Acuitlapilco near the city of Tlaxcala (pages 196–7). Plumed serpents, sculptured columns, elaborate friezes and freestanding warriors adorn the main house, which was designed to promote tourism and to commemorate the glorious achievements of pre-Hispanic civilizations.

Opposite *Yaxcopoil, Yucatán* Imposing entrance to a sisal hacienda. Moorish-style double archways of this type are particular to Yucatán.

Post-Conquest architecture in Mexico has been characterized by its eclecticism. Decorative elements from the Old World, introduced over centuries, have been consistently absorbed and reinterpreted by Mexican builders. The Baroque period gave full expression to the creative imagination, and resulted in lavish displays of stucco, tiles, ironwork, carved stone and gilded wood. The sobriety of the early nineteenth century was followed during the Porfirian era by renewed enthusiasm for extravagance and embellishment; until the Revolution of 1910, *haciendas* and town-houses drew freely and often incongruously on neo-classical, Renaissance, Tudor, Gothic Revival, Victorian romanesque, neo-Baroque, Moorish and Art Nouveau sources.

In the wake of Bauhaus teachings, architects and designers from Europe and the USA have increasingly rejected surface decoration in favour of functionalism and purity of form. For Adolf Loos, Czech-born architect and polemical precursor of the modern movement, ornament was 'tantamount to crime': 'The evolution of culture', he stated in 1908, 'is synonymous with the removal of ornament from utilitarian objects'. In Mexico, after 1940, Luis Barragán drew much of his inspiration from the stark, monastic simplicity of early colonial constructions. Yet, despite international trends and Loosian rigorism, untutored builders without number retain a fondness for ornamentation and flamboyant detail; they also have the patience and skill to make their aspirations a reality. It is cheaper to construct a fence, a tomb or a stair-rail than to buy one that has been commercially produced, and more challenging to personalize it than to leave it plain. Even when erecting a house, an individual does not need to seek planning permission: there are no regulations to curb the builder's flights of creative fancy.

Exuberance and lack of inhibition find expression in strongly coloured and patterned walls, as shown in Part 1. Sometimes streets are enlivened by imaginative hand-painted advertisements and signs (see page 44). Mary Barton, who commented so irascibly on Mexico's colour range, was in better – if patronising – mood when describing naive paintings in the capital. The following description, published in 1911, could apply in many rural towns today: 'An odd thing that strikes me at once in the city is that the posters are not printed and pasted on walls but painted thereon by hand, and are generally of an immense size. Most of them are, of course, appalling, but immensely enterprising and painstaking; and some are very comical, either from intention – as in the case of the advertisement of a gramophone which was depicted as belching forth its comic song in front of the Sphinx, whose head was tilted back in a paroxysm of laughter, showing one immense tooth – or by accident, when the perspective of a shop finds a vanishing point a few yards away, or a figure at least eight feet high displays a towering collar round a head of less than normal size, and stands on little patent leather feet of not more than six inches in length.'

Churches and chapels are often decorated and wholly maintained by the people who use them. Over decades, façades have been painted and interiors refurbished to suit local tastes. Neon lights have proved popular in several regions, where they now surround ornate colonial altars and illuminate Baroque saints and angels. Such innovations do not always find favour with resident or visiting priests.

Unlikely juxtapositions also occur in many rural homes. In his book *The Architecture of Mexico: Yesterday and Today*, published in 1969, Hans Beacham recalled a telling incident: 'Nearly twenty years ago, during a rainstorm in the Isthmus of Tehuantepec, we were invited to take shelter and refreshments with an old shepherd and his wife. His thatched hut was warm, dry and impeccably clean. On the wall hung a small plaster statue of the Virgin, painted pink and blue. Illuminated by a candle, she was standing on a half-moon. To her left hung a bright chromium-plated hubcap from a 1935 Plymouth. The combination, though startling, did not seem incorrect. Today these improbable decorative juxtapositions are still startling but also continue to seem correct. This is because the foreigner can rarely become jaded in Mexico. In fact he is in danger of expecting to be surprised at every turn. Such an attitide would limit his point of view and do the Mexicans an injustice.'

Ironically, in the southwestern part of the USA, such eclecticism is now fashionable and stylish. Tim Street-Porter's photographs, taken in the late 1980s for *Casa Mexicana*, show how Mexico's vernacular architecture, decoration and vibrant colour combinations have served as an inspirational catalyst for artists and designers in Los Angeles and other cities. A striking example is the home shared by the artist Jon Bok and Robert Lopez, who curates for the Luz de Jesus gallery and performs on stage as 'El Vez'. Found objects, which include gleaming hubcaps, are freely combined with *papier-mâché* skeletons, carved wooden saints and masks from Mexico. Adolf Loos would not be amused.

264 San José Ozumba, Puebla Stable wall of stone, dated 1754, on a Jesuit hacienda. Tiny pebbles, pressed into mortar, form a series of designs. Seen here are plant forms, a human figure and the sun.

265 San Roque, Puebla Hacienda water-tower with an access ramp. By turning a wheel at the top, mules drew water for the needs of the estate.

266△ 267▽

266 Santa Mónica, Zacatecas *Conical silos for storing grain produced on the* hacienda. **267 San Isidro Buensuceso, Tlaxcala** *A carved stone face watches over the doorway of a house.*

268△ 269▽

268 *Tlacoaleche, Zacatecas* Massive grain
silos. 269 *Calvillo, San Luis Potosí*
Bricks, elegantly stacked around mounds
of wood, wait to be fired.

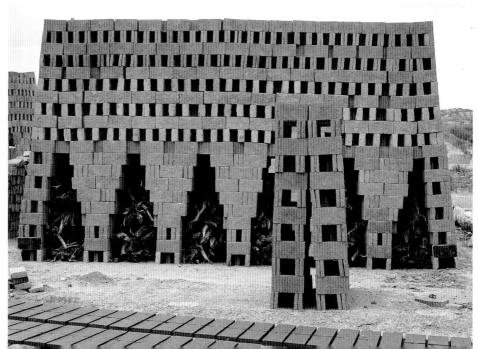

270△

270 **Tepeyahualco, Puebla** Atrium wall enlivened by decorative battlements.
271 **San Pedro Apóstol, Oaxaca** Family tomb. 272 **Pizarro, Puebla** An observation tower dwarfs the church and adjoining hacienda buildings.

271△

272▷

273 Santa María del Tule, Oaxaca
Waterspouts in the form of coyotes.
274 Acatlán, Puebla A papier-mâché *ram*
surveys the street from the flat roof of a
potter's house.

273△ 274▽

275 *Alamos, Sonora* Perforations pattern metal doors with swan motifs. 276 *Mérida, Yucatán* Mould-made birds of painted plaster embellish a house-fence.

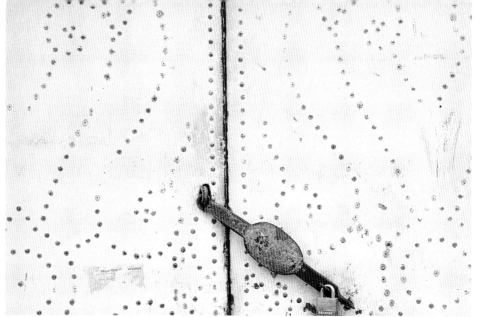

275△ 276▽

277△

277 **Acatlán, Puebla** Fish of papier mâché
with cane armature. 278 **San José
Amealco, Mexico State** White fish pattern
the recently constructed patio pavement of
an old hacienda. 279 **Topolobampo,
Sonora** Archway with a metal adornment
in the shape of a goat.

278△

279▷

281 △

The snake is a frequent element in popular art. **280 Alamos, Sonora** *Garden sculpture of plaster.* **281 and 282 Cholula, Puebla** *Stair-rails fashioned from industrial cement.*

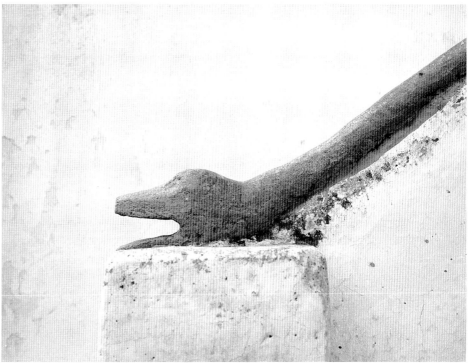

◁280   282 △

283 Santiago de Anaya, Hidalgo Otomí *house of* maguey *(Mexican agave). The door, like the roof-frame, is made from the* quiotes *(woody flower stalks) of this invaluable plant. Cheap to build and ideally suited to the local climate, such houses are now becoming rare (see also pp. 64–5).*
284 San Juan Buenavista, Mexico State *Bales of fodder, stacked up by farmers, take the form of a building.*

283 △ 284 ▽

285 El Carmen Tequexquitla, Tlaxcala
Nahua house made from sun-dried rye stalks arranged in layers (see also ill. 9).
286 Tlacoyalco, Puebla *Cattle fodder stacked up in the form of a house.*

285△ 286▽

287△

Decorative details of originality and charm are often to be found in rural churches and graveyards. The dead are frequently honoured with ornate and imaginative monuments. **287 San Sebastián Teitipac, Oaxaca** Church entrance.

288▷

288 Otumba, Mexico State Moorish-style mausoleum of recent date.

289 △ 290 ▽

289 Santo Domingo Jalieza, Oaxaca Contemporary buildings occasionally incorporate pre-Hispanic or colonial elements. Here, an ancient Zapotec stone carving serves as a window lintel in a wall of adobe bricks. **290 Acuitlapilco, Tlaxcala** Although twentieth-century Mexicans often take great pride in their pre-Hispanic past, few have made their admiration as manifestly clear as the late Salazar Monroy, author, inventor and antiquarian. Anxious to promote tourism in the state of Tlaxcala, he financed an architectural complex commemorating pre-Hispanic achievements. The house, richly patterned and brightly painted, is now maintained by the Department of Tourism.

291△   292▽

291 *and* **292 Acuitlapilco, Tlaxcala**
Balcony and fence, from the house built by
Salazar Monroy, recall Baroque styles of
architecture.

197

293 Santiaquillo, Zacatecas *Waste is rare in rural Mexico. Here, an old bus has its life extended when it is incorporated into a fence.*

294 Atlixco, Puebla *Stable door in Art Deco style fashioned from scrap metal.*

GLOSSARY

adobe
Sun-dried mud brick.

alfarje
Ceiling of many small pieces of wood worked into a repetitive interlacing design, often found in Moslem and *mudéjar* work.

alfiz
Rectangle of moulding embracing an arch, found in Moslem, *mudéjar* and Plateresque work.

altiplano
High plateau of central Mexico.

Amusgo
Indian language-group living in adjoining areas of Guerrero and Oaxaca (approximate population: 18,500).

architrave
In classical architecture the lowest division of the entablature resting immediately on the abacus of the column.

artesonado
Wooden ceiling with coffers (*artesones*, usually square or polygonal) sunk between its beams.

atrio
Atrium: large walled forecourt of a Latin-American church.

azotea
A flat roof where residents can work and walk about.

bajareque
Wattle-and-daub.

ballcourt
The pre-Conquest ballgame (*tlachtli*) had a cosmic significance. Courts were I-shaped.

barrio
Neighbourhood; ward or precinct.

bejuco
Generic term for diverse plants with long, flexible stalks; liana or vine.

brutalism
Uncompromisingly modern style of architecture which dates from the mid-1950s and works in raw and exposed materials such as concrete.

calpulli
Náhuatl term: territorial unit; subdivision in a pre-Conquest town.

casco
Main buildings and administrative centre on a *hacienda* or landed estate.

charrería
Mexican horsemanship.

charro
In Mexico, this term is applied to horsemen.

chinampa
Indian cultivation plot surrounded by waterways; 'floating garden'. Much used before the Conquest by the Aztec inhabitants of Tenochtitlan, this form of agriculture persists today around Xochimilco. From the Náhuatl *chinamitl*.

Chinantec
Indian language-group living in northwestern Oaxaca (approximate population: 67,000).

Chol
Maya sub-group living in northern Chiapas and adjacent settlements in Tabasco (approximate population: 94,000).

cincolite
(Also *cincolote*). Type of corncrib found on the *altiplano*. From the Náhuatl *colotli*.

coatepantli
Náhuatl term: circuit wall of an Aztec sacred enclosure, often crested with carved serpents.

codex or *códice*
Pre-Conquest or post-Conquest manuscript.

comal
Earthenware griddle for cooking tortillas. From the Náhuatl *comalli*.

corbel
Weight-bearing projection of stone.

corredor
Corridor; gallery around a patio.

criollo
Creole: colonial and 19th-century term for someone of Spanish parentage born in Spanish America.

cuezcomate
(Also *cuescomate*, *coscomate*, *cozcomate*). Vasiform corncrib commonly found in Morelos, with a clay base and a roof of *zacate* (grass). From the Náhuatl *cuez* and *comitl* (jar, or pot).

dentils
Toothlike classical ornament used in cornices.

ejido
Lands held under communal tenure.

encomienda
A royal grant of Indian labour to a Spanish settler; tract of land inhabited by natives bound in *encomienda*.

encomendero
Grantee: possessor of an *encomienda*.

entablature
The upper part of an order of architecture, comprising the cornice, frieze and architrave.

entrepiso
Entresol, mezzanine.

espadaña
Wall pierced with arches in which bells are hung.

fresco
Mural painting on plaster.

gabled roof
Roof in which the pitch falls in two directions from the centre of the building.

grille
An ornamental arrangement of metal bars forming a screen, partition or railing.

guardapolvo
Skirting of paint along the base of walls.

hacendado
Hacienda-owner.

hacienda
Large landed estate, usually a plantation given over to agriculture or cattle-raising.

henequén
Sisal (*Agave fourcroydes*).

hipped roof
(Also hip roof). Roof in which the pitch falls in four directions.

Huichol
Indian language-group residing high in the Sierra Madre where the states of Jalisco and Nayarit meet (approximate population: 49,500).

jagüey
Man-made pool, tank or cistern.

jamb
Side piece of a window or door.

Lacandón
Indian language-group residing in the Chiapas rainforest. Beliefs and practices are inherited from the ancient Maya (approximate population: 300).

lámina
Corrugated sheet-metal.

lintel
Horizontal stone slab or timber beam spanning an opening, and supported on columns or walls.

maguey
Popular term for the Mexican agave,

which includes some 200 species.

marl
Rich earth or clay.

Maya
The culture of the ancient Maya is described on pages 12–15. Although the contemporary Maya family includes a number of peoples in Mexico and other countries, the term is specifically applied to people of the Yucatán Peninsula (approximate population: 630,000).

Mayo
Indian language-group living in southern Sonora and northern Sinaloa (approximate population: 55,500).

Mazahua
Indian language-group belonging to the Otomí family; resident in Mexico State and adjoining areas of Michoacán (approximate population: 181,000).

Mendicant
Term, meaning begging, applied to the religious orders dependent on alms (in 16th-century Mexico the Franciscans, Dominicans, Augustinians and, later, the Carmelites).

merlon
A single battlement, the short section of a military parapet between two gaps.

mestizo
Mexican of mixed Indian and European descent.

metate
Flat stone on which maize, *cacao* and other foodstuffs are ground with the aid of a *metlapil*. From the Náhuatl *metlatl*.

metlapil
(Also *meclapil*). Elongated cylindrical stone used during grinding operations on a *metate*. From the Náhuatl *metlapilli*, literally 'son of the *metate*' (*metlatl* and *pilli*).

milpa
Maize plot.

Mixtec
Indian language group from northern and western Oaxaca. Before the Conquest, the Mixtec excelled as builders, goldsmiths and codex painters (approximate population: 282,000).

mudéjar
Art in Moslem or Moslem-influenced style for Spanish Christians, chiefly from the 13th to the 15th centuries.

Nahua
Indian language-group living in Puebla,

Morelos, Tlaxcala and a number of other states (approximate population: 1,317,000).

Náhuatl
Language spoken by the Aztec and some of their neighbours; today Náhuatl is spoken by the Nahua.

nopal
Prickly pear cactus (*Opuntia ficus indica*). From the Náhuatl *nopalli*.

ocotillo
Popular term for *Tamarix gallica* and other species of spiny shrub found in desert areas of Mexico.

otate
Generic term for Mexican bamboo or cane. From the Náhuatl *otatl*.

Otomí
Indian language-group living in Mexico State, central Hidalgo and some other regions (approximate population: 280,000).

patio
Inner courtyard.

peninsular
Colonial term for a Spaniard inhabiting Mexico but born in Spain.

petate
All-purpose mat of interwoven palm or rushes. In many indigenous homes it serves as a seat during the day and a bed during the night. *Petates* can also be used to carry loads, and to wrap corpses for burial. From the Náhuatl *petlatl*.

Plateresque
A form of rich surface ornament in Spanish architecture used in both Gothic and Renaissance building. The term is derived from *platería* (silverwork).

plaza
Public square.

Poblano
Pertaining to the state of Puebla.

Porfiriato
The Porfirian era, under Porfirio Díaz, which lasted from 1876 to 1911.

portales
Arcades, porticoes, colonnades surrounding *plazas*.

Presidencia
Seat of local government, town hall.

pueblo
Small Indian village.

pulque
Alcoholic beverage made from the sweet sap of *Agave atrovirens* and also from

some other species of *maguey*.

pulqueria
Bar or tavern where *pulque* is sold.

Purépecha
(Also Tarascos). Indian language-group living in the north of Michoacán (approximate population: 92,700).

Puuc
Late Classic style of architecture characteristic of Maya sites in the Puuc region of southwestern Yucatán.

quiosco
Bandstand.

rajuela, rajueleado
Small pebbles positioned between adobe bricks.

reja
Grille.

repartimiento
System of draft labour.

retablo
Reredos: decorated panels rising above the back of an altar.

shingle
Thin wooden slab used in the manner of a roofing slate or tile.

sierra
Mountain range.

solar
Yard.

tapanco
Loft. From the Náhuatl *tlapanco*.

tapial
(Also *tapia*). Wall construction of earth (sometimes clay or mortar and rubble) rammed between boards and allowed to harden.

Tarahumara
Indian language-group from the mountains of southwestern Chihuahua (approximate population: 57,200).

tejamanil
Shingle.

temascal
Indigenous sweathouse for steam baths. From the Náhuatl *temazcalli*.

teocalli
Náhuatl term: temple atop a pyramid.

tequitqui
Post-Conquest art style (relief sculpture in particular) using European motifs combined with an Indian sense of pattern. First used in this sense by José Moreno Villa, *tequitqui* is the Náhuatl term for 'one who pays tribute', or 'a subject person'.

tezontle
(Also *tesoncle*). Type of volcanic stone, porous and either grey or reddish in colour. From the Náhuatl *tetzontli*.

tinacal
Building where *pulque* is made.

tortilla
Thin, unleavened pancake of ground, dried maize.

Totonac
Indian language-group living in southeastern Veracruz and northern Puebla (approximate population: 186,000).

trapiche
Sugar mill; small workshop.

troje
Granary.

Tzeltal
Indian language-group, of the Maya family, living in central Chiapas (approximate population: 212,600).

tzompantli
Náhuatl term: skull rack.

Tzotzil
Indian language-group, of the Maya family, living in highland areas of central Chiapas (approximate population: 132,000).

wattle-and-daub
Framework of poles and interwoven twigs smeared over with mud or clay.

zacate
Popular term for grass, straw and the stalks of some grain-producing plants. From the Náhuatl *zacatl*.

Zapotec
Indian language-group living in Oaxaca. Before the Conquest, the Zapotec excelled as builders and ceramists (approximate population: 347,000).

zócalo
Main square.

BIBLIOGRAPHY

Agarwal, Anil
Mud, Mud: the Potential of Earth-based Materials for Third-World Housing, London 1981.

Ajofrín, Francisco de
Diario del viaje que . . . hizo a la América Septentrional, en el siglo XVIII, el P. Fray Francisco de Ajofrín, Madrid 1958.

Baird, Joseph A.
The Churches of Mexico, 1530–1810, Berkeley, Calif., 1962.

Bakewell, Peter J.
Silver Mining and Society in Colonial Mexico: Zacatecas 1546–1700, Cambridge 1971.

Bardou, Patrick and Varoujan Arzoumanian
Arquitecturas de adobe (Tecnología y Arquitectura), Barcelona 1979.

Barthelemy, Ricardo and Jean Meyer
La casa en el bosque, Michoacán State 1987.

Bartlett, Paul Alexander
Haciendas of Mexico: An Artist's Record (intro. Gisela von Wobeser), Niwot, Colorado, 1990.

Barton, Mary
Impressions of Mexico with Brush and Pen, London 1911.

Baxter, Sylvester
Spanish-Colonial Architecture in Mexico (10 vols.), Boston 1901.
La arquitectura hispano colonial en México (intro. and trans. Manuel Toussaint), Mexico City 1934.

Bazant, Jan
Cinco haciendas mexicanas: tres siglos de vida rural en San Luis Potosí (1600–1910), Mexico City 1975.

Beacham, Hans
The Architecture of Mexico: Yesterday and Today (intro. Mathias Goeritz), New York 1969.

Boils, Guillermo
Las casas campesinas en el porfiriato, Mexico City 1982.

Brading, David A.
Miners and Merchants in Bourbon Mexico, 1763–1810, Cambridge 1971.
Haciendas and Ranchos in the Mexican Bajío: León 1700–1860, Cambridge 1978.

Brocklehurst, Thomas Unett
Mexico To-day: a country with a great future, And a glance at the prehistoric remains and antiquities of the Montezumas, London 1883.

Calderón de la Barca, Frances
Life in Mexico during a Residence of Two Years in that Country, London 1843.

Cali, François
The Art of the Conquistadors, London 1961.

Carrillo, Rafael A.
El arte barroco en México desde sus inicios, hasta el esplendor de los siglos XVII y XVIII, Mexico City 1987.

Caso, Alfonso
Reyes y reinos de la Mixteca, Mexico City 1977.

Celorio, Gonzalo, Jorge Loyzaga, Margarita Mansilla
Arquitectura fantástica, Mexico City 1991.

Cervantes de Salazar, Francisco
México en 1554 . . ., Mexico City 1939.

Champlain, Samuel de
The Works of Samuel de Champlain (6 vols), Toronto 1922–36.

Chavero, Alfredo, et al.
'La Conquista de México : Lienzo de Tlaxcala', *Artes de México* 51/52, año XI., Mexico City 1964.

Chevalier, François
Land and Society in Colonial Mexico: the Great Hacienda, Berkeley, Calif., 1963.

Codex Florentino
See Sahagún, Bernardino de

Codex Mendoza (Bodleian Library, Oxford)
Fac. edn, 3 vols (ed. James Cooper Clark), London 1938.

Codex Zouche-Nuttall (British Museum, London)
Fac. edn (intro. Arthur G. Miller), New York 1975.

Coe, Michael D.
The Maya, Harmondsworth, Middx., 1977.
Mexico (revised and enlarged edition), London 1984.

Conquistador Anónimo
Relación de algunas cosas de la Nueva España y de la gran Ciudad de Temestitlán México, escrita por un compañero de Hernán Cortés, Mexico City 1941.

Cook de Leonard, Carmen (ed.)
Esplendor del México Antiguo (Vol. 2), Mexico City 1959.

Cortés, Hernán (Fernando, or Hernando)
Cartas de relación, Mexico City 1969.
Letters of Cortés (trans. and ed. F. A.

MacNutt; 2 vols.), London and New York 1908.

Cortina, Leonor (ed.)
'La Talavera de Puebla', *Artes de México* nueva época 3, Mexico City 1989.

Cosío Villegas, Daniel
Historia moderna de México: La República Restaurada; El Porfiriato (2 parts: 10 vols.), Mexico City and Buenos Aires 1955–72.

Dethier, Jean, et al.
Des Architectures de Tierre, ou l'Avenir d'une Tradition Millénaire, Paris 1981.

Díaz del Castillo, Bernal
Historia verdadera de la conquista de la Nueva España (intro. and notes Joaquin Ramírez Cabañas), Mexico City 1967.
The True History of the Conquest of New Spain (trans. and annotated A. P. Maudslay; 5 vols), London 1908–16.

Durán, Fray Diego
The Aztecs: the History of the Indies of New Spain (trans. and annotated by Doris Heyden and Fernando Horcasitas), New York 1964.

Edwards, Emily
Painted Walls of Mexico from Prehistoric Times until Today (photographs by Manuel Álvarez Bravo), Austin, Texas, 1966.

Escobedo, Helen, et al.
Mexican Monuments: Strange Encounters, New York 1989.

Fathy, Hassan
Architecture for the Poor, Chicago 1973.

Figueroa Ochoa, Fidel
'Parque educativo: Ex-hacienda de Pantitlan, "Pabellón el Universo"' (Ph.D. diss.), Facultad de Arquitectura, U.N.A.M., Mexico City 1989.

Gage, Thomas
The English-American his travail by sea and land, or a new survey of the West Indies, London 1648.
Thomas Gage's Travels in the New World (ed. J. Eric S. Thompson), Norman, Texas, 1969.

García Maroto, Gabriel
Arquitectura popular de México (intro. Enrique Yañez), Mexico City 1954.

Garza Tarazona de González, Silvia
Codices genealógicos: Representaciones arquitectónicas, Colección Científica No. 62, Arqueología, Mexico City 1978.

Gibson, Charles
The Aztecs under Spanish Rule: A History of the Indians of the Valley of Mexico, 1519–1810, Stanford, Calif., 1964.

Grossi, Oscar and Angel Tuero
Arquitectura popular, Buenos Aires 1977.

Guzmán Ríos, Vicente
Arquitectura y magueyes, Xochimilco, Mexico c. 1982.

Hernández Xolocotzi G., Efraim
Graneros para maíz en México a través de los siglos, Chapingo, Mexico, 1965.

Heyden, Doris
Origen de un símbolo: mito y simbolismo en la fundación de México-Tenochtitlan (Colección Distrito Federal 22), Mexico City 1988.

Heyden, Doris and Paul Gendrop
Pre-Columbian Architecture of Mesoamerica, London 1988.

Ingle, Marjorie
The Mayan Revival Style, Salt Lake City, Utah, 1984.

Instituto Nacional de Bellas Artes
La Arquitectura de la Epoca Porfiriana, *Cuadernos de Arquitectura y Conservación del Patrimonio Artístico* No. 7 (Serie Monografías), Mexico City 1980.
Arquitectura Vernácula, *Cuadernos de Arquitectura y Conservación del Patrimonio Artístico* No. 10 (Serie Ensayos), Mexico City 1980.

Katzman, Israel
Arquitectura del siglo XIX en México, Mexico City 1973.

Kelemen, Pál
Mediaeval American Art, New York 1946.
Art of the Americas: Ancient and Hispanic, New York 1969.
Baroque and Rococo in Latin America, New York 1977.

Kubler, George
Mexican Architecture of the Sixteenth Century (2 vols), New Haven, Conn., 1948.
The Art and Architecture of Ancient America: the Mexican, Maya and Andean Peoples, Harmondsworth, Middx., 1962.

Kubler, George and Martin S. Soria
Art and Architecture in Spain and Portugal and their American Dominions 1500 to 1800, Harmondsworth, Middx., 1959.

Landa, Diego de
Relación de las cosas de Yucatán (ed. Alfred M. Tozzer), Cambridge, Mass., 1941.

Leander, Birgitta
Herencia cultural del mundo náhuatl, Mexico City 1972.

Lengen, Johan van
Manual del Arquitecto descalzo: Como construir casas y otros edificios, Mexico City 1982.

Lienzo de Tlaxcala
See Chavero et al., Alfredo.

Lira Vásquez, Carlos
Para una historia de la arquitectura mexicana, Mexico City 1990.

López Morales, Francisco Javier
Arquitectura vernácula, Mexico City 1989.

Lowry, Malcolm
Dark as the Grave wherein my Friend is Laid, London 1969.

Lumholtz, Carl
Unknown Mexico: A Record of Five Years' Exploration Among the Tribes of the Western Sierra Madre . . ., New York 1902.

McAndrew, John
The Open-Air Churches of Sixteenth-Century Mexico: Atrios, Posas, Open Chapels, and other Studies, Cambridge, Mass., 1965.

Magdaleno, Mauricio, et al.
'Haciendas de México', *Artes de México* 79/80, Mexico City c. 1969.

Margain, Carlos R.
Pre-Columbian Architecture of Central Mexico, *Archaeology of Northern Mesoamerica: Part I*, vol. 10 of *Handbook of Middle American Indians* (series ed. Robert Wauchope), Austin, Texas, 1965.

Marquina, Ignacio
Arquitectura prehispánica, Mexico City 1964.

Matos Moctezuma, Eduardo
The Great Temple of the Aztecs: Treasures of Tenochtitlan (trans. Doris Heyden), London 1988.

Maza, Francisco de la
La Ciudad de México en el siglo XVII, Mexico City 1985.

Mendieta, Gerónimo
Historia eclesiástica indiana (4 vols.), Mexico City 1945.

Meyer, Michael C. and William L. Sherman
The Course of Mexican History, New York 1991.

Miller, Mary Ellen
The Murals of Bonampak, Princeton, N.J., 1986.

Monroy, Salazar
Forja colonial de Puebla, Puebla City 1946.
Fuentes coloniales de Puebla, Puebla City 1946.
Jambajes artísticos de Puebla, Puebla City 1965.

Morley, Sylvanus G.
The Ancient Maya (revised by George W. Brainerd), Stanford, Calif., 1956.

Motolinía (Toribio de Benavente)
Motolinía's History of the Indians of New Spain (trans. and annotated by Francis Borgia Steck), Washington, D.C., 1951.
Memoriales, Mexico City 1903.

Moya Rubio, Victor José
La vivienda indígena de México y del mundo, Mexico City 1988.

Nierman, Daniel and Ernesto Vallejo
La hacienda en México, Mexico City 1990.

Obregón, Gonzalo, et al.
'La Ciudad de Puebla', *Artes de México* 81/82, año XII, Mexico City 1966.

O'Gorman, Patricia
Patios and Gardens of Mexico, New York 1979.
Tradition of Craftsmanship in Mexican Homes, New York 1980.

Oliver, Paul
Dwellings: The House across the World, Austin, Texas, 1987.

Paso y Troncoso, Francisco del (ed.)
Papeles de Nueva España, Madrid 1905–06.

Poniatowska, Elena
'Luis Barragán', *Todo México (Tomo 1)*, Mexico City 1990.

Porter, Eliot and Ellen Auerbach
Mexican Churches, Albuquerque, N.M., 1987.

Pozo Rosillo, Pauline del and Matilde Cabrera Ipiña de Corsi
'Las haciendas potosinas', *Artes de México* 189, año XXII, Mexico City c. 1973.

Prieto, Valeria (ed.)
Vivienda campesina en México, Mexico City 1978.

Redfield, Robert and Alfonso Villa Rojas
Chan Kom, Washington, D.C., 1934.

Relación de Michoacán
Published as *The Chronicles of*

Michoacán (trans. and ed. Eugene R. Craine and Reginald C. Reindorp), Norman, Texas, 1970.

Robertson, Donald
Pre-Columbian Architecture, New York 1963.

Rudofsky, Bernard
Architecture without Architects, New York 1964.
Streets for People: A Primer for Americans, New York 1969.

Sahagún, Fray Bernardino de
General History of the Things of New Spain (trans. and ed. Arthur J. O. Anderson and Charles E. Dibble), 13 parts, Santa Fe, N.M., 1950–82.

Sanford, Trent Elwood
The Story of Architecture in Mexico, New York 1947.

Santamaría Francisco, J.
Diccionario de mejicanismos, Mexico City 1959.

Sartorius, Carl
Mexico. Landscapes and Popular Sketches, London 1858.

Sayer, Chloë
Arts and Crafts of Mexico, London 1990.

Schávelzon, Daniel (ed.)
'Las representaciones de arquitectura en la Arqueología de América' (Vol. 1: *Mesoamerica*), Mexico City 1982.

Schele, Linda and Mary Ellen Miller
The Blood of Kings: Dynasty and Ritual in Maya Art, Fort Worth, Texas, 1986.

Secretaría del Patrimonio Nacional
Vocabulario Arquitectónico Ilustrado, Mexico City 1976.

Shipway, Verna Cook and Warren Shipway
The Mexican House Old and New, New York 1960.

Sidaner, Jean-Gérard
De barro y de otate, Guerrero State 1988.

Simpson, Lesley B.
The Encomienda in New Spain, Berkeley, Calif., 1960.

Soustelle, Jacques
Daily Life of the Aztecs on the Eve of the Spanish Conquest (trans. Patrick O'Brian), Stanford, Calif., 1970.

Standley, Paul C.
'Trees and Shrubs of Mexico', in *Contributions from the United States National Herbarium*, 23, Washington, D.C., 1969.

Stephens, John Lloyd
Incidents of Travel in Central America, Chiapas, and Yucatan, London 1841.

Stierlin, Henri
Living Architecture: Mayan, London 1964.
Living Architecture: Ancient Mexican (trans. Marion Shapiro), London 1968.

Street-Porter, Tim
Casa Mexicana: The Architecture, Design, and Style of Mexico (intro. Marie-Pierre Colle), New York 1989.

Toor, Frances
A Treasury of Mexican Folkways, New York 1947.

Torquemada, Fray Juan de
Monarquía indiana (ed. Salvador Chávez Hayhoe), Mexico City 1943.

Torre, Mario de la (ed.)
Haciendas: Herencia mexicana, Mexico City 1988.

Toussaint, Antonio
El Plat=eresco en la Nueva España, Mexico City 1971.

Toussaint, Manuel
Arte mudéjar en América, Mexico City 1946.
Paseos coloniales, Mexico City 1962.
Colonial Art in Mexico (trans. and ed. Elizabeth Wilder Weissmann), Austin and London 1967.

Turner, John Kenneth
Barbarous Mexico (intro. Sinclair Snow), Austin, Texas, 1990.

Tylor, Sir Edward B.
Anahuac: or Mexico and the Mexicans, Ancient and Modern, London 1861.

Vaillant, George C.
Aztecs of Mexico: Origin, Rise and Fall of the Aztec Nation (revised by Suzannah B. Vaillant). Harmondsworth, Middx., 1978.

Valdés, Luz Ma. and Ma. Teresa Menéndez
Dinámica de la población indígena (1900–1980), Mexico City 1987.

Villanueva, Benjamín
Arquitectura popular de Sinaloa, Sinaloa, Mexico, c. 1980.

Vogt, Evon Z.
The Zinacantecos of Mexico: a Modern Maya Way of Life, New York 1970.

Vogt, Evon Z., et al.
Ethnology: Parts 1–2, vols. 7–8 of Handbook of Middle American Indians (vol. ed. Evon Z. Vogt; gen. ed. Robert Wauchope), Austin, Texas, 1969.

Wauchope, Robert
: *Modern Maya Houses: A Study of their Archaeological Significance*, Washington, D.C., 1938.

Wobeser, Gisela von
: *La formación de la hacienda en la época colonial: el uso de la tierra y el agua*, Mexico City 1989.

Wolf, Eric R.
: *Sons of the Shaking Earth: The People of Mexico and Guatemala – Their Land, History and Culture*, Chicago 1974.

Yampolsky, Mariana
: *La casa en la tierra*, Mexico City 1981.
: *La casa que canta*, Mexico City 1982.
: *La raíz y el camino* (intro. Elena Poniatowska), Mexico City 1985.
: *Tlacotalpan* (intro. Elena Poniatowska), Mexico City 1987.
: *Estancias del Olvido* (intro. Elena Poniatowska), Mexico City 1987.
: *Haciendas poblanas* (intro. Ricardo Rendón Garcini), Puebla City 1992.

Yarwood, Doreen
: *The Architecture of Europe: The Middle Ages 650–1550* (Vol. 2), London 1992.

ILLUSTRATION ACKNOWLEDGMENTS

Unless otherwise specified, all photographs are by Mariana Yampolsky.

Drawing after the historian Fernando Alva de Ixtilxóchitl (1568–1648) 9; Anonymous 16th-century drawing by Indian artist: 19 (*below*); Engraving by Auber, 19th century: 13 (*above*); *Codex Florentino* (1564–65): 10, 11, 16 (*above*), 23 (*above*); *Codex Magliabecchiano* (*c.* 1553): 37 (*above*); *Codex Zouche-Nuttall* (*c.* 1300–1500): 16 (*below*), 36 (*below left*); Map illustrating the Second Letter of Hernán Cortés to Charles V in a Latin edition by Pietro Savorgnano, Nuremberg 1524: 8; Drawing by Emilio Dondé, 1898: 28 (*above*); Justino Fernández, from *Paseos coloniales* by Manuel Toussaint, Mexico City 1962: 22; *Hart Picture Archives, Vol. 1: A Compendium*, New York 1976: 27; William H. Holmes, *Archaeological Studies among the Ancient Cities of Mexico: Anthropological Series*, Vol. 1, Chicago 1895–7: 12 (*below*); Drawing by Jorge Huft: 31; *Lienzo de Tlaxcala* (1550–64); copy of lost original made in 1773: 17, 37 (*top*); Archivo Enrique Díaz, Archivo General de la Nación, Mexico City: 158; Archivo General de la Nación, Mexico City: 19 (*above*), 32; Fototeca del Instituto Nacional de Antropología e Historia, Mexico City: 28 (*below*), 30; *La Litografía en México en el siglo XIX*, Mexico City 1934: 26; Drawing after Sylvanus G. Morley, *The Ancient Maya* (rev. George W. Brainerd), Stanford, Calif., 1956: 13; Illustrations by Salvador Ortega, from *Forja colonial de Puebla*, by Salazar Monroy: 21; *Relación de Michoacán* (1539–41): 15; Carlos Lira Vásquez, *Para una historia de la arquitectura mexicana*, Mexico City 1990: 23 (*below*); 25; Robert Wauchope, *Modern Maya Houses: A Study of their Archaeological Significance*, Washington, D.C., 1938: 35; Illustration by Whymper, from *Mexico To-day* by Thomas Unett Brocklehurst, London 1883: 29; Mariana Yampolsky: 34 (*above* and *below*), 36 (*above* and *bottom right*).

INDEX

Numbers in *italic* refer to captions to black and white illustrations; those in **bold** refer to captions to colour illustrations.